The Actor Alone

To the memory of Joseph Campbell,
because he taught us to follow our bliss,

and to Paul Baker,
because he taught us to believe in
the vision of our own landscape

The Actor Alone

Exercises for Work in Progress

by CLAUDIA N. SULLIVAN

with a foreword by
PAUL BAKER

McFarland & Company, Inc., Publishers
Jefferson, North Carolina, and London

Every attempt has been made in this book to avoid the use of gender biased language. There are times, however, when the language itself is limited. Therefore the use of such terms as *actor, he* and *himself* is not intended to refer only to the masculine gender. My use of these terms reflects universal gender orientation. — C.N.S.

Excerpts from *Death of a Salesman* by Arthur Miller, copyright 1949, renewed ©1977 by Arthur Miller, used by permission of Viking Penguin, a division of Penguin Books USA Inc.

Excerpts from *Death of a Salesman* by Arthur Miller, copyright 1949, renewed ©1977 by Arthur Miller, used by permission of Viking Penguin, a division of Penguin Books USA Inc.

Excerpts from *Glass Menagerie* by Tennessee Williams, copyright 1945 by Tennessee Williams and Edwina D. Williams, reprinted by permission of New Directions Publishing Corporation.

British Library Cataloguing-in-Publication data are available

Library of Congress Cataloguing-in-Publication Data

Sullivan, Claudia N., 1952–
    The actor alone : exercises for work in progress / by Claudia Sullivan.
      p. cm.
    Includes bibliographical references and index.
    ISBN 0-89950-842-1 (sewn softcover : 55# alk. paper) ∞
    1. Acting. I. Title.
PN2061.S78   1993
792'.028 — dc20
                        92-51093
                        CIP

Manufactured in the United States of America

McFarland & Company, Inc., Publishers
Box 611, Jefferson, North Carolina 28640

ACKNOWLEDGMENTS

The research for this book began many years ago while I was a student at the Dallas Theatre Center under the direction of Paul Baker.

I am deeply indebted to the faculty of the Dallas Theatre Center during the years 1972 through 1976. In particular I would like to thank Mary Sue Jones, Robyn Flatt and Sally Netzel. Ms. Netzel is largely responsible for developing the exercises which appear in this book. Her pragmatic approach to the study of acting, combined with the integration of abilities philosophy, provided an acting curriculum which I have used throughout the past fifteen years of college teaching.

The creative atmosphere at the Dallas Theatre Center during the early to middle 1970s fostered the imaginative and artistic growth of many students and professional theatre practitioners. Paul Baker and the faculty of the graduate department of theatre at Trinity University in San Antonio, Texas, were responsible for creating in the Dallas Theatre Center a place for ideas to grow and a place to take creative risks. Each day I realize the benefits of my study there and I am thankful for that opportunity.

This project would not have been possible without the help of my many students over the past years. Most especially, I would like

v

to thank all the students enrolled in the spring 1992 acting classes at Schreiner College in Kerrville, Texas, for their participation in these acting exercises. I wish especially to thank Katharine Armstrong, Karen Barrett, Roby Conner, Stephen Dyer and Laura Naber, whose works appear in this book. Their work in progress will, no doubt, provide examples for future acting students.

The photographs presented in this book are the work of professional photographer Linda Blase, student photographer Obdula Gonzales, and Lane Tait of College Relations at Schreiner College.

Finally I would like to thank Patricia Hutchins, instructor of art at Schreiner College, for her visual designs. Her work has expanded the integrated arts view of this book.

TABLE OF CONTENTS

ACKNOWLEDGMENTS v

FOREWORD *(by Paul Baker)* ix

PREFACE xi

INTRODUCTION 1

CHAPTER I: WHAT IS ACTING? 9

    The Acting Craft: Craft vs. Art 11

CHAPTER II: THE ELEMENTS OF ACTING 17

    The Integration of Abilities 20

        Rhythm 23

        Space 32

        Sound and silence 35

        Movement 39

        Line and direction 43

        Silhouette 45

        Texture and color 47

        Integration vs. Stanislavski's System 49

CHAPTER III: EXERCISES FOR CREATIVE
 GROWTH 55
 The Ten Line Exercise: The Six Studies 59
  The word study 61
  The sound study 64
  The visual study 65
  The movement study 66
  The choice study 67
  The ten line study 68

CHAPTER IV: THE ACTOR WORKING ALONE 73
 Dramatic Analysis 73
  Word study 76
  Sound study 76
  Visual study 87
  Movement study 92
  Choice study 97
  Ten line study 100

CHAPTER V: WORK IN PROGRESS 111

CHAPTER VI: THE ACTOR AT WORK 143
 The actor at work alone 146

APPENDIX 151

NOTES 155

BIBLIOGRAPHY 159

INDEX 163

FOREWORD

This book is a watershed—a guide to and summary of the thousand ways an actor can find and develop his character when working alone, a thousand ways for any artist to find his creative center. *The Actor Alone* summarizes the universal artistic act, the universal secrets used by master artists since the time of the first cave drawings.

In this book Claudia Sullivan splits the artistic atom by dissecting and breaking open the relationship of the five senses as experienced through the universally accepted vocabulary of the elements of form: space, movement, rhythm, shape, texture, sound and silence, line and color. Each of these elements of form is defined as it functions in the creative act. *The Actor Alone* simplifies and illuminates the actor's exercise using each element of form.

Claudia Sullivan has further simplified the task of the actor working alone by recommending an additional ingenious method: After analyzing the six dimensions of a play (plot, characterization, idea, language and sound, visual elements, and form and spirit), Sullivan outlines a wonderful new approach, the Ten Line Exercise. The Ten Line Exercise suggests that the actor working alone "select a minimum number of lines which focus on high points in the life of the character on stage." The technique is applied in extensive analyses of several selected plays demonstrating for the actor how to use this idea when studying a script.

I believe *The Actor Alone* will become a most useful tool for any artist who is searching for a way to enter any creative work.

Paul Baker
February 1993

PREFACE

My first memory of being on stage was when I was four or five years old. It was my first ballet recital, and I was one in a long line of other four- and five-year-olds. Our tutus were pink and we wore crowns that sparkled with rhinestones and sequins. We marched across the stage and performed our pliés and our tondus, trying to stay in time with the music and watch our teacher in the wings at the same time. When our performance was finished we did our curtsies and the line headed offstage — all except me. Miss Naomi hadn't told us the audience would applaud at the end of our dance. I was so surprised by the applause that at first I was frightened. Then by some instinct I curtsied again. Still more applause, this time mixed with laughter. Since all the others had left the stage I knew the applause was for me. I had discovered a great truth, not unlike the feeling Pavlov's dog must have had at the presentation of food upon the sound of that bell. I continued to curtsy and the audience continued to applaud and laugh and I loved it! The more I curtsied, the more the audience applauded and laughed. Finally, my ballet instructor appeared and grabbed me by the arm, dragging me off the stage (I was curtsying all the while). That was my first experience on the stage and I was hooked. Now I couldn't get enough.

At the age of eleven I enrolled in children's theatre classes at the Casa Manana Theatre School in Fort Worth, Texas, under the direction of Sharon Benge. When I was cast as Peter Pan the director kept saying, "Be bigger. You're bigger than life! Be *bigger!*" I tried to be taller, fatter, louder and larger than anyone else on stage. It wasn't what the director was looking for. Perhaps I was too young and inexperienced to understand what "Bigger!" meant. I certainly didn't know the right questions to ask. I did what I was told to the best of my ability and tried to be a good actor.

In high school I was cast as Auntie Mame. Again I heard the directions, "Be bigger. Be larger than life." This time I knew to ask, "Bigger how? Larger in what way?" And so I moved in a grand style. I gestured in a more sweeping manner. I was on the right track.

I continued to study acting in college, but it was not until I was in graduate school at the Dallas Theatre Center that I came into contact with a creative genius in the surprising form of Paul Baker. Because I lived in Texas and had studied acting for more than ten years, I was well acquainted with Paul Baker and his unconventional approach to the art of the theatre. There were stories of him as the department chair at Baylor University in Waco, Texas, and his unusual theatre. There was considerable disagreement between Baker and the administration over the upcoming production of Eugene O'Neill's *Long Day's Journey into Night*. The administration wanted him to cut questionable words from the dialogue. He refused. They insisted. He resigned and so did most of the drama and speech staff. Trinity University in San Antonio welcomed Baker and his staff with open arms. Later they built an entire theatre complex for him designed around his suggestions on style and convention of the physical theatre itself.

His association with the Dallas Theatre Center began in the late 1950s. He had an idea for a theatrical environment which would serve as an artistic mecca for artists from around the world. His theatre, more European in concept than American, would focus on the creative integrity of the individual artist rather than seek to produce commercially successful plays grown more out of a need to make money than creative honesty.

A board of directors was formed, money was pledged and the Dallas Theatre Center was born. World renowned architect Frank Lloyd Wright was brought on to design the theatre with Baker's suggestions for innovative staging. Some felt that Wright knew everything about architecture but little about the needs of a theatre.

Baker knew theatre but little about architecture. The two had a stormy working relationship but the theatre was completed in 1959, shortly after Wright's death.

Baker's reputation grew as a leader in new movements in American theatre. He supported new playwrights and encouraged European designers and directors to visit his theatre and share ideas and techniques. The Dallas Theatre Center became a place for ideas to grow. It became associated with Trinity University through Baker's direction. He served as theatre department chair at Trinity and managing director of the Dallas Theatre Center, spending much of his time traveling from one campus to the other.

I came to the Dallas Theatre Center in 1972 and for the first time I began to see the making of theatre as an integrated activity in which the artistic abilities of each person were acknowledged and supported.

Baker wrote about his personal approach to the making of theatre in *Integration of Abilities: Exercises for Creative Growth*. This book, based on a series of lectures presented at Trinity University, outlines his strong feelings about teaching theatre, the importance of creative integrity, the path to artistic growth and the power of the imprint of one's sensory awareness in childhood.

It was through Baker's exercises for creative growth and the highly supportive atmosphere of the Dallas Theatre Center that I began to adopt a different approach to acting.

Sally Netzel, a protégé of Baker, instructor in the graduate school and member of the resident company of actors at the center, developed a series of exercises for her students in advanced acting. Her exercises were based on many of Baker's teachings and other more conventional acting instruction techniques used in the past. Sensory awareness and sense memory were combined with integration of abilities. Netzel had learned from her own experience a practical approach to acting, too. "Sometimes directors won't be very helpful. Sometimes they won't know how to help you in finding your character or honing your skills. More often than not they won't have the time to help you," she advised.

Netzel combined some practical steps for character study with some accepted techniques from Stanislavski, Grotowski and Artaud and presented them in a manner consistent with Paul Baker's integration of abilities philosophy.

This experience provided me with the right questions to ask of directors and myself as I worked on a role. It helped me to understand the creative process as it is channeled through the individual artist, whether visual artist, writer, designer, choreographer, director or actor.

I continued to study acting and later I moved on into play directing. Now, with a doctorate and years of experience, I teach both. I never lost that love for acting. I never forgot how magical it felt to stand on a stage with the lights in my eyes and look out over the audience. And I never forgot the sound of the applause.

Perhaps your interest in acting began in a similar way. Or perhaps your interest in acting began by accident at a later age. Were you filling in for someone who dropped out of a high school production? Were you painting scenery at the local community theatre when you decided to try your hand at acting? Or were you one of those people who always liked to tell stories at family gatherings and finally someone said, "You ought to be an actor!" and you decided to try it? Or did you always want to be a professional actor on stage, on television or in film? Whatever your particular case, you are not alone.

Each year in the United States thousands of people, young and old, professional and amateur, act in little theatres, community theatres, experimental theatres, university theatres, children's theatres, and professional theatres. All these theatres have one thing in common: they need actors. Good actors, actors willing to learn, actors willing to experiment and take creative risks, actors that are responsible and dependable and enthusiastic, and actors who are willing to share of themselves and their own creative potential. This is the acting craft—the making of theatre.

So—Listen! Work like a dog! Justify! Make every-thing internally real to yourself! Serve the play-wright, the director, your fellow actors and conse-quently the audience!

— UTA HAGEN

INTRODUCTION

Paul Baker opened Baylor University Theater in 1941 with this:

This theatre is dedicated to the young at heart, to the dreamer, to the imaginative creator of beauty for others. This theatre exists to challenge the best in its devotees — the living, the inspired part of each of their lives. It aims to reach out to the roots of our soil and our people . . . to interpret, to portray what is truth — to select what is good, what gives joy, what is real.

This theatre starts with the needs of a people, and reaches out through the child, the student, the man — touching each with its varied endeavor, showing each the nobility of man, his weakness, his greatness.

This theatre attempts to be new in its concept, to offer only the best to its advocates. May it stand firm, sure of its footing, resolved to hold fast through the treacherous times for its friends and neighbors, to our basic dreams and realities.

The doors are open; bring in your thought, bring in your rarest desire, bring in your best. Here you may find expression and growth; here you may find a gateway to service; here you may find real understanding.

To those who want to keep alive the dream and help to weave a finer dream for the future, we dedicate this theater.

Enter — it is yours.[1]

Baker read the same words at the opening of the Ruth Taylor Theater at Trinity University in 1966.

Paul Baker stands vigilant in his desire to pursue artistic integrity and to pass that legacy on to his students, followers and even to those audience members who come to witness his directing efforts.

Much of this book is directly related to the teachings of Paul Baker. All of it is indirectly linked to his unique philosophy and his supportive teaching. It is therefore important to introduce this book with an overview of his life and work in the theatre. Although he has worked primarily in the southwestern United States, his influence has been felt internationally through the teachings of his students and followers, the productions performed by his protégés and his associations with artists from Europe and the Orient.

Paul Baker grew up in the flat and dusty landscape of west Texas. This usually infertile land proved especially rich for Baker, who at an early age developed a sense of self-definition based on his own responses to the land, its color, its line and shape, its texture and silhouette.

These images burned deep in Baker's consciousness, and many years later, while studying drama at Yale University, he recalled his childhood responses to the land. He found what he later termed his landscape. "Landscape" for Baker was one's personal vision, one's unique response to stimuli.

By 1952 Baker had become professor of drama at Baylor University in Waco, Texas. That summer he journeyed to Paris with a group of drama students. For years he struggled against the formal traditions of theatre. He was challenged by the restrictions he felt denied true creativity. Finally, his formless ideas began to take shape when he confronted the visual artworks of Picasso, Rouault, Chagall and Bissiere in the Paris Museum of Modern Art.

His memory of the early responses to the environment somehow triggered new insight into the style, form and intent of the great masters of modern art. He experienced a transformation of his own style which began to shape the manner in which he approached the making of theatre.

Traditional theatre for Baker was "a concept of people in a box speaking to other people in their box." Baker demanded more of the experience. Graduate student Elizabeth Wear Stecker recorded his ideas.

These artists seem to be seeing an object from many directions at the same time. They have broken away from painting an upright on a horizontal plane at eye level. These paintings are not restricted by the picture frame; they have emerged from it to the viewer. How? Look at the stark simplicity of Picasso's background. Rouault, simplicity of form and close grouping of bodies surrounded by wide expanse. The floor. Picasso's floor there is important, heavily designed. . . . Can it be that the excitement folks in balcony seats always claim has something to do with the floor? By ramping the floor, could we make the audience see the actor as against the sky?[2]

Baker made a profound discovery. Upon his return to Baylor he set out to redefine theatre as he knew it and had practiced it. His production of Shakespeare's *Othello* included not one Othello but three actors portraying psychological traits of the same character. Costumes, scene designs and makeup were unified in theme and style. He used a ramped stage so that the actor's movements were intensified. Critics raved and hailed him and his theatre as "progressive" and "stunning."

Baker's commitment to a vital and innovative theatre included an integrated study of painting, dance, music and sculpture. He was especially interested in fostering the growth of new plays and new playwrights. His association with playwright Eugene McKinney began at Baylor and continued at Trinity University. McKinney's play *A Different Drummer* was acclaimed and was produced for CBS-TV's "Omnibus." In its productions at Baylor, on CBS and at Trinity, *A Different Drummer* involved actors such as Clu Gulager and his wife Marian (both of whom were Baylor students), Carole Cook (a Baylor student and Broadway star) and Edward Hermann (a television and film star). Set designer Virgil Beavers used ideas inspired by paintings by Piet Mondrian for the production.

During his tenure at Baylor, Baker worked with Charles Laughton and Burgess Meredith. Meredith was so intrigued by Baker's ideas that he agreed to come to Waco to perform in Shakespeare's *Hamlet* in a production directed, of course, by Baker.

In the late 1950s Baker began a turbulent relationship with architect Frank Lloyd Wright. The Dallas Theatre Center was to be the only public theatre Wright ever designed. Baker oversaw the plans and insisted on specific theatrical requirements, sometimes conflicting with Wright's ideas. The Dallas Theatre Center opened in 1959. Wright never knew that the plans for the theatre had been altered to include a freight elevator linking the lower level scene shop with the main stage theatre. Baker insisted that a theatre must have access between shop and stage. Wright adhered to his organic idea that a theatre, like those of ancient Greece, must be a place of manual work. Wright was ill and wheelchair bound at his last inspection and never noticed the elevator, conveniently disguised by a variety of backstage theatre paraphernalia. Dozens of students at the Dallas Theatre Center have sworn they saw Wright's ghost during late night rehearsal periods. Theatre myths hold that all theatres are haunted in some way.

The 1964 production of *Journey to Jefferson*, an adaptation of William Faulkner's novel *As I Lay Dying* by Baker associate Robert Flynn, won the Special Jury Prize for "best total production" in the Theatre of Nations competition in Paris, France. Years earlier Flynn and Eugene McKinney had adapted Thomas Wolfe's *Of Time and the River* for the stage. That production won critical acclaim in *The Christian Science Monitor*, *Time*, and *Life*.

Perhaps Baker is best known for his association with playwright Preston Jones and the original staging of his plays *The Last Meeting of the Knights of the White Magnolias*, *The Oldest Living Graduate*, and *Luann Hampton Overlander Laverty*. The Texas Trilogy, as the plays were called, skyrocketed the career of Preston Jones to a successful run at the Kennedy Center and Broadway. Once again Baker's efforts in support of new playwrights paid off.

In 1972 Baker synthesized the ideas he had been developing over the past several decades and published *Integration of Abilities: Exercises for Creative Growth*. In this book he outlined his philosophy for discovering one's own approach to the creative process and artistic work. A course by the same title was offered as part of the undergraduate curriculum at Trinity University and was required for all students.

There can be much resistance to Baker's style of working. It is difficult and time consuming. It does not promise a quick fix, immediate results or certain success. Some who do not understand the implications of his theory or who have never studied it claim that it merely rehashes Stanislavski's theories in new words. This accusation is not true.

Baker's approach is innovative. It focuses on the total theatre: design elements, directing styles, acting methods, writing styles and multi-media techniques. More important, Baker believes in the innate gift of all who wish to learn. He discounts the idea that so-called "natural talent" is the only prerequisite to success or stardom. He advocates the idea of being true to oneself first rather than the more popular belief in giving the critics what they want.

As he stated in the address delivered in 1941 and in 1966, the theatre is a place of ideas, hope and understanding. The dream of a better theatre is the dream of a better life.

These are his ideas as passed on from one generation of students who became teachers to another generation of students and teachers. I have been a student and now as a teacher in my own right I pass on my ideas, my interpretation of what I have learned. You are students who will someday pass on what you have learned, through either your work, your words or your efforts.

We actors stand by our present performance. . . . We are as immediate as the moment. We give you our feelings and hope you will return yours. We ask for acceptance; we are your servants.

Scratch an actor and underneath you'll find another actor.

—LAURENCE OLIVIER

I
WHAT IS ACTING?

The theatre is a mirror of life. The actor plays out the roles of all of us. He is what Carl Jung calls "the collective unconscious." We find ourselves in the reflection he presents.

Through a study of acting we learn about ourselves as we are, as we would have ourselves to be and as we have been. We act our dreams, our fears, our fantasies and our mythic rituals. We awaken each morning and play out the role of mother, doctor, student or thief, but that is not the same as acting for performance—though both types of roles share common elements. In so-called "real life" we do more than represent the character. We *are* the character, existing in a world in which we can respond spontaneously and without regard to technique or artistic flow.

In performance acting, acting a dramatic character on a stage for an audience, a whole series of technical, creative and artistic skills comes to play in a single moment.

In order to know how to act one must first know what acting is and understand what tasks are involved in the process of acting.

The following are principles of acting which both define it and indicate a psychological and methodological approach to it.

9

• Acting is a process. The actor is continuously learning to act. Acting is not a technique which once mastered never changes; each time the actor begins a new role the process begins again. Certain elements of acting remain the same, but the educational and experiential process of acting is ongoing. The great teacher and director Constantin Stanislavski states that "An actor grows as long as he works. . . . Over a period of years of study [an actor] learns to follow a right course on his own . . . and having learned to do his work properly he becomes a master of his art."[3]

• Acting is an act of creation. Each time an actor performs a role he strives to create something new. The true act of creation is one which brings something new into being, something that did not exist in the same way before. It is important that actors look upon their work as an act of creation, not as a reenactment of something that has been done before.

• Acting is a learned activity. Acting is not mysterious or magical. It can be learned but it takes time, dedication, hard work, and acceptance of numerous setbacks. Some actors learn quickly and seem naturally suited to the process of acting; others struggle and progress slowly and with difficulty. Nonetheless, a person can learn to act if he is willing to look inside and outside himself, thereby becoming a true student of life.

• Acting can be an art. Peter Brook said in his book *The Empty Space*, "An actor prepares, he enters into a process that can turn lifeless at any point. He sets out to capture something, to make it incarnate."[4] Since acting is an act of creation, each actor should strive for a level of artistic quality. Reach for the highest ideals of your work; don't settle for less, and never for what will just suffice.

• Acting is not limited to the confines of a play or the physical limitations of a theatre. I am often amused by beginning acting students who claim that they cannot act. As proof of this statement they say, "I've never been in a play in my life." But they are wrong. Each of us acts every day at work, at home and in our relationships. We "act" as if we are happy when we are really sad, we "act" as though we like someone whom we find a bore. This behavior I call life acting. It is from life acting that we can gain information for stage or character acting. Stage acting can take place in many non-theatre settings such as lofts, churches, parks, classrooms, museums and other places where plays or improvisations are performed.

• Acting does not always have to be believable. Not all characters are crafted from reality; sometimes they are meant as symbols, sometimes as parodies. A role from a musical comedy is less believable than a role from Chekhov or O'Neill because the reality of the context is different. Sometimes the nonrealistic characterization can heighten the meaning. In acting there is a difference between being believable to an audience and acting as though you believe your character.

• Acting should be performed with a sense of personal integrity. Your acting is your own. Call it your own and it belongs to no one else. Good or bad, believable or not, your acting is an extension of the work and effort you have put into its creation. Don't settle for less. Don't give in to the easy way out and the "cookie-cutter" style of acting. As Peter Brook states,

> These carbon-copy imitations are lifeless. Repetition denies the living. It is as though in one word we see the essential contradiction in the theatre form. To evolve, something needs to be prepared and the preparation often involves going over the same ground again and again. Once completed, this needs to be seen and may evoke a legitimate demand to be repeated again and again. In this repetition lie the seeds of decay.[5]

Believe in yourself. Believe in your work and let it stand for itself.

• Acting is a journey, not a destination. Many actors think that once the play has opened the creative work is complete. It is not. Each performance is different, each audience is different, and each actor is different. Even when you must perform a role many times a week for many months you are still learning and changing and becoming. The journey is never over. In acting you are always evolving and changing.

The Acting Craft: Craft vs. Art

When you think of a craft, what comes to mind? Needlecraft or macramé? Woodworking or jewelry making? What about furniture making, bookbinding, glass staining, basketweaving, painting, dancing, and acting? Is acting a craft or an art, or can it be both?

A craft is something done with skill and ingenuity. It is learned with particular steps or techniques as part of the process. We usually associate crafts with manual dexterity. But dancers and actors often refer to themselves as craftsmen. They speak of "perfecting my craft." Acting can be a craft, a learned activity in which steps or techniques are mastered to a level of professionalism. If acting is a craft, how or when is it properly described as an art? One dictionary definition of art is "the skillful arrangement of means for the attainment of some end, especially by human endeavor as opposed to natural forces." If acting is an art, the actor-as-artist must skillfully arrange or rehearse certain aspects of his characterization for performance. Does not the actor-as-craftsman do the same?

Another definition goes farther to state that art must exist "in a creative form to produce works that have form or beauty, esthetic expression of feeling." So acting as art is a higher level than acting as craft and of an aesthetically different quality.

Aristotle and the Greeks of the fifth century established the principle that art must imitate nature. Nature set the ideal and perfect standard for human representation. The Greeks were working toward a sense of reality, but their perception of reality (believability) was different from the twentieth century perception. Standards of reality and believability change with time, culture and aesthetic preferences. Modern actors must understand this in order to free themselves to play the roles of any period or style.

Joel G. Fink, professor of theatre at the University of Colorado, states in his article "Too, Too Solid Flesh" that "*acting* is defined as: the shaping of personal responses to the stimuli of 'given circumstances,' through the use of an expressive self-instrument, for the purpose of theatre."[6]

The craft of acting can be learned by almost anyone with the time, opportunity, motivation and intelligence to persevere and study the task at hand. Anyone can act, and act well! There are certain skills and techniques that can be mastered. Actors should approach their work like craftsmen but aspire to be artists. An actor referring to himself as a craftsman deserves no less praise or respect than one who calls himself an artist. But it is the actor-artist who has gone beyond the level of learning the craft to a plane of artistic and aesthetic purity. As artist, the actor has created a role which possesses qualities of beauty, form, and completeness. The artistic performance transcends the level of the ordinary or the merely acceptable. It rises above and speaks in a voice larger than itself; it goes beyond the performance to touch on greater matters—the human condition and the significance of life. Acting may be either craft or art. Certainly the craft of acting must be mastered prior to the art.

In his book *Acting Without Agony* Don Richardson illustrates the art of acting.

> I'll teach you how to approach the art of acting without driving yourself crazy. I'll give you principles and a way to plan your work. To be a professional you must be good all the time and sometimes better; that means working with a plan. The sculptor builds an armature before he models his clay, the painter makes sketches, the architect a blueprint. Only the actor thinks he can do his work through inspiration alone. You wouldn't hire an inspirational plumber.[7]

The actor who studies his craft and approaches the level of artistic work becomes a changed person as a result of his work. The actor becomes a reflection of himself—his experiences, perceptions, attitudes and working process. As he takes on the role he combines the reflection of himself with that of the character, thus offering a new world view in his persona on stage. The ideas of the playwright, the character (which has a life of its own within the context of the play) and the actor present a unique world view to the audience. Joseph Chaikin states,

> An actor should strive to be alive to all that he can imagine to be possible. Such an actor is generated by an impulse toward an inner unity, as well as by the most intimate contacts he makes outside himself. When we as actors are performing, we as persons are also present and the performance is a testimony of ourselves. Each role, each work, each performance changes us as persons. The actor doesn't start out with answers about living—but with wordless questions about experience. Later, as the actor advances in the process of work, the person is transformed. Through the working process, which he himself guides, the actor recreates himself.
> Nothing less.
> By this I don't mean that there is no difference between a

stage performance and living. I mean that they are absolutely joined. The actor draws from the same source as the person who is the actor.

In former times acting simply meant putting on a disguise. When you took off the disguise, there was the old face under it. Now it's clear that the wearing of the disguise changes the person. As he takes the disguise off, his face is changed from having worn it. The stage performance informs the life performance and is informed by it.[8]

To act a passion well, the actor never must attempt its imitation, until his fancy has conceived so strong an image, or idea, of it, as to move the same impressive springs within his mind, which form that passion, when it is designed, and natural.

—Aaron Hill

II

THE ELEMENTS OF ACTING

Creative growth is important to all human beings and essential to the actor. The creative spark is inherent in every individual, yet man is continuously searching for new ways to develop and express his creativity. This book invites the actor to undertake an exploration and cultivation of his own creative spark in the development of a character for the stage. Ideally the actor's work is done with others within the context of rehearsals and performances of the role before a live audience. Many times, however, the actor is working alone either in preparation for an audition or outside of rehearsal periods.

The exercises presented here are for the actor working without the constant and direct leadership of director, teacher, coach or audience. After all, much of the preparatory work done by actors is in solitude.

There are many existing methods or systems of developing a character for the stage. The Stanislavski system or Method as it is called in the United States is arguably the most often used and most famous of all actor training techniques. Elements of the Stanislavski Method are similar to those presented in this book. Both approaches call for introspection, awareness of working methods, intense character analysis and a step by step procedure of character development.

Other methods or approaches include Grotowski and his "poor theatre" approach; the psychoanalytic, Stanislavski-based method of Lee Strasberg, the late director of the Actor's Studio; and other more traditional approaches.

Each system offers a unique approach to the process of acting. For some actors certain systems work well while other systems can seem ineffective. Different roles from varied styles of production require a different methodology. What worked well for the character of Juliet from *Romeo and Juliet* may not be helpful in the development of Blanche from *A Streetcar Named Desire*.

Actors may find that their needs change according to stages of development in their careers.

The works of Constantin Stanislavski and his system have provided a foundation from which all modern acting flourishes. Despite the controversy which has surrounded it, the Stanislavski System continues to be the pervasive technique taught to young actors today. The American interpretation of the Stanislavski System as practiced by Lee Strasberg, Harold Clurman, Sanford Meisner, Stella Adler and a host of others provides still more depth and imagination for the modern actor to utilize. Many novice actors are confused by the terms *System* and *Method*. The *System* refers to Stanislavski's exercises for character development including the "magic if," the emotion memory, the method of physical actions, sense memory, etc. It is amazing that we are still, after some fifty years, reinterpreting and re-analyzing the writings and accounts of lectures by Stanislavski.

The language barrier and obstacles such as time, distance and outright misquotation of Stanislavski have contributed to the confusion and controversy. A prime example of a source of confusion is the term *bit*. For years followers and students of the Stanislavski System were told by their Russian teachers to study the *bits* of the scene. Actors were advised to break their scenes into units so that they could better analyze and prepare the role. *Bit* was actually a mispronunciation of the word *beat*. This example illustrates how easily and how often the words of Stanislavski were misused, mispronounced and misinterpreted altogether.

The *Method* refers to the Americanized version of the System, which is primarily practiced at the Actor's Studio. The exercises and intensely psychological, introspective approach of the Method have fueled most of the controversy. Some contemporary actors, teachers of acting and directors are adamant in their mistrust and dislike of the Method. Don Richardson states, "I don't believe in the Stanislavski 'Method.' I also don't believe you have to become a drunk to play one, or shoot yourself up to play a drug addict. . . ."[9]

He goes on to state that from his experience in directing actors and teaching acting the Method does not work. Others claim that the Method is responsible for the mumbling style so representative of American actors of the 1950s and 1960s, especially such actors as Marlon Brando and James Dean. In defense of the Method Peter Brook states,

> Years ago, the Actor's Studio came into being to give a faith and continuity to those unhappy artists who were being so rapidly thrown in and out of work. Basing a very serious and systematic study on a portion of Stanislavski's teachings, the Actor's Studio developed a very remarkable school of acting. . . . The Method Actor was trained to reject cliché imitations of reality and to search for something more real in himself. He then had to present this through the living of it, and so acting became a deeply naturalistic study.[10]

The contributions of Uta Hagen, Robert Benedetti, Sanford Meisner, Joseph Chaikin, Jerzy Grotowski and others have added to the wealth of approaches and systems from which the modern actor can explore, investigate, and create a working and believable character for the stage.

This book presents one approach which takes advantage of any and all other methods without limiting the individual actor to any particular one. A combination of exercises integrates techniques with the actor's self-awareness.

Self-awareness may be defined as an actor's sensitivity to and awareness of his own reactions to the artistic elements present in his environment. In other words, how does the actor respond to the elements of space, rhythm, sound and silence, color and texture, silhouette, line and direction and movement? Some of these reactions may come out of childhood memories or experiences, or previously unconscious reactions to elemental stimuli. The actor's self-awareness should not be confused with the deeply psychological and introspective exercises which were part of the Lee Strasberg Actor's Studio program.

Some who read this book and utilize the exercises may find similarities between the integration approach and Stanislavski's exercises. Surely there are similarities, but the integration approach, of which the ten line exercise is a part, employs a different point of view.

Stanislavski did his original work during the first two decades of the twentieth century. His influence is international and pervasive. There is no contemporary acting approach that does not use elements of Stanislavski's System. The ten line exercise, however, combines many different techniques and approaches. It does not rule out any prior experience. It invites each actor to make the best use of any and all training he may have had before. The ten line exercise integrates for the actor that which works in each unique situation.

Every actor should have at his or her disposal a means through which to explore and refine a character from *any* play for *any* director. It is not uncommon for an actor to confront a new working method or style for which he cannot find an answer to the old question: How do I approach this character? Consider that a director may ask an actor to perform in a style to which he is unaccustomed. Where is the actor to go for advice and guidance? The ten line exercise provides a way for the actor to find answers to his own questions if and when the director may be unavailable or unhelpful.

The Integration of Abilities

Paul Baker presents an effective philosophy of self-awareness in his book *Integration of Abilities*, in which he discusses how he arrived at his theory, its uses and its applications to acting, directing, design and creative writing. Baker served as chairman of the department of drama at Baylor University, and later at Trinity University and the Dallas Theatre Center. During his tenure at Trinity a course in the integration of abilities was required for all undergraduates to improve and inspire their creativity. Baker also served as arts consultant for the Arts Magnet School in Dallas, Texas. He is now retired but still directs and leads seminars and workshops.

The nucleus of the integration philosophy lies in the individual's reactions to his particular environment and the stimuli provided in that environment. Baker classifies certain elements of experience in the creative growth process such as rhythm, space, sound and silence, line and direction, movement, silhouette, and texture and color. Through a study — an integration of one's awareness to these stimuli — the actor begins a new phase of creative maturation. "I think we all have these feelings in relationship to the earth and to the sky and to sound and to silence; to movement and rhythms, no matter where we are from, no matter what our background. We build on these stimuli; we live out these experiences."[11]

To achieve this goal of creative maturity a dialogue with oneself must be established. A necessary step in the development of such a dialogue is a reexamination of certain childhood experiences, both mental and physical.

> Integration of abilities starts at that point when we were very young, before we had words to put the feelings together, or words to destroy the feelings. It starts at where we were when we were very alone and very private people.
>
> There are many people who also had those experiences, to a larger or smaller degree, who can share them with us in their books and their writings: Thoreau, in his writing of nature; Frank Lloyd Wright, in his marvelous feeling for the reality of space inside a building, the functional value of space; Craig and Appia, in their relationship to space in the theatre, in applying these same principles out of nature to the theatre, to its space, to its movement, to its direction and its rhythms; Jean-Louis Barrault, in his feeling, in the discovery of silence as an enormous living element within space; impressionist and cubist painters, in the various movements that have grown out of those very alive ideas in each period of history which is left to us in essence; the Bauhaus Group, out of which grew Moholy-Nagy, with his excellent works *Vision in Motion* and *The New Vision*, which have shown the essence of and the relationship between texture, line, movement, color, form related to space; the Greek playwrights, in the grandeur of their poetry, the strength of the emotion and the vitality of the mind.[12]

One cannot escape one's environment or its imprint on the minds. In the brief years of childhood, the pattern for all future reactions, perceptions and responses is established. In the unconscious memories of sounds, rhythms, various spaces and colors are recorded. These recorded data are in turn correlated to other factors found in daily life and in turn opinions, ideas, values, and prejudices are formed.

In a world of patterns and similarities, we search to discover some unique quality of existence in which we can express our own ideas. This perception of the philosophy of the integration of abilities allows us, in any walk of life, to awaken the latent creative talents which are present in each individual. This book applies to the actor who seeks to create a fresh, new dramatic character on the modern stage.

The present day actor must have the courage to explore unique and often unknown talents and to avoid the quick results so often sought by novice or inexperienced actors, who frequently observe a convenient pattern or style of acting and adopt it, never realizing the uniqueness of their own abilities.

> No amount of self-analysis will substitute for good diction and controlled movement; no amount of diction practice or fencing lessons will substitute for self-knowledge and developed instincts. The good actor must have both to be exciting. If the actor is merely competent, he is a dime a dozen and capable only of imitation and clichés.[13]

Creative expression often resides in a world beyond words. The actor must explore beyond the words and examine the feelings and emotions of both himself and the character he wishes to portray. He must employ all his senses to understand and apply his imagination. The artist must, in an effort to become more aware and sensitive, analyze the elements which compose the total of any performance. The artist's technique is composed of perceptible tools which must be cultivated and activated to make a creative and solitary statement. Each actor will have a different set of tools, a different set of stimuli, a different background, and different interests.

Michael Chekhov in *To the Actor* referred to "the richness of the psychology" and went on to state that

> a sensitive body and a rich, colorful psychology are mutually complementary to each other....
> You will achieve it by constantly enlarging the circle of your interest. Try to experience or assume the psychology of persons of other areas by reading period plays, historical novels or even

history itself. While doing so, try to penetrate their thinking without imposing upon them your modern points of view, moral concepts, social principles, or anything else that is of a personal nature.[14]

The actor should work toward a level of objectivity when approaching any character. If the actor is allowed to view the character in a play only through a subjective mind he will destroy his own inventive talents. Sensitivity is achieved through the objective experience of relating to other circumstances, ideas, and emotions through the physical response to these stimuli classified as *elements*.

The integration of acting abilities synthesizes these creative elements so that the actor may attain his maximum potential.

RHYTHM

Early in the fetal stages of human life begins a rhythm of life, a rhythm which from its earliest moment possesses a certain unique pulse. This rhythm, which is the beat of the heart, becomes stronger and more pronounced, until at the time of birth it is independent of the mother's rhythm. At birth the rhythm of the heart is thrust into an alien space and is coupled with a new rhythm, that of the breath. These two rhythms constitute the life-beat that permeates the lifetime existence of the individual. The unconscious motion of the heartbeat serves as a constant rhythmic force within the body and maintains organic order. Breathing dictates a subconscious, and often conscious, timing to our movements, speech and even thinking.

As individuals grow and mature their movements take on specific rhythmic patterns. Each person has a unique manner of walking, gesturing and subsisting at rest. Individual movement patterns exist within broader social contexts. These contexts include proxemics and kinesics.[15]

The third rhythmic organization is motor rhythm, the rhythm of the body as it moves through space in time. In constant conflict to maintain balance against the force of gravity, the body cuts through space and achieves motion (see Fig. 1).

The fourth and final mode of rhythmic organization is emotional. As emotions rise and subside emotional rhythms are created. These are usually manifested in some form of verbal, vocal, or physical manner.

Fig. 1. Doris Humphrey exhibits a rhythm of motion (courtesy Morgan & Morgan Publishers).

Within this structural pattern are varieties of rhythm. Emotional and physical responses occur in each type of rhythmic pattern. Auditory rhythms include such repetitive sounds as the chopping of wood, the shuffling of feet on a city street, the rhythm of waves breaking against the shore, the hustling rhythm of cars speeding along a freeway at workday's end, or the rhythm of men marching in a military parade. Examples of visual rhythm may exist in an architectural design such as the Empire State Building or the Guggenheim

Museum, in the flight of a seagull, in the juxtaposition of earth and sky as visible in the horizon, or in the form exhibited by a bonsai tree (see Fig. 2).

Varying rhythms can also be found in certain classifiable areas: the passage of the seasons or the character of different cities, periods of history, occupations, and times of day.

This breakdown of the elemental rhythms enables humans to develop an awareness to rhythmic patterns existing in everyday life, and to use that awareness to the enrichment of the total self. Rhythm is inherent in every living thing.

Dancers and musicians accept this element readily. Doris Humphrey aptly states,

> Rhythm so permeates every aspect of human beings, and indeed, of the known world, that it might be compared to the ambience of existence, like the water in which the fish moves, the water and the fish having rhythmical differentials, too, of each is quite aware. . . . Rhythm is the great organizer. Habits of accent form to hold an organism together, patterns of rhythmical shape lend sense and sensibility to anarchistic, chaotic, a menace to all organization.[16]

The organization provided by rhythm was evident in early human culture. Rhythm so permeated language, ritual dances, interactions with nature, and attitudes toward a supreme being that the actor's (or shaman's) rhythmic sense played a great role in daily life. This seemingly uncomplicated approach to the understanding of rhythmic forces has slowly been repressed within the increasing complexity of modern civilized societies. In the process of societal evolution the importance of rhythm has been diminished and man's awareness to it has been numbed. At one time the steady beat of the drum was man's motivating rhythm; now, in the hustling cities, it is difficult, at times even impossible, to identify a single dominant rhythm. The complexity of metropolitan rhythms often forces the urban dweller into habitual patterns that conform to the nebulous ebb and flow of the environment's many elements.

Every individual is faced at one time or another with the choice of abiding by a pattern or breaking away from its monotony and creating something unique and rhythmically inventive. This decision is particularly important to the actor on the modern stage.

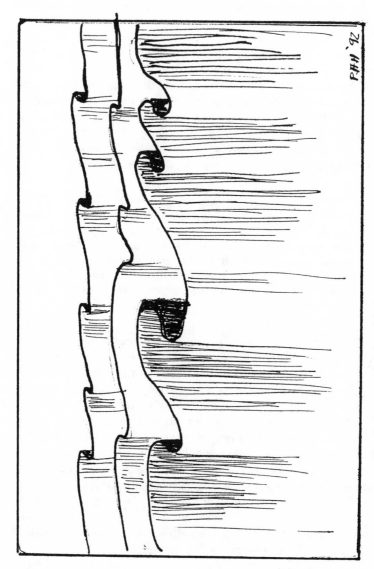

Fig. 2. An example of visual rhythm (courtesy Patricia Hutchins).

Actors frequently reduce the dramatic impact of a production by playing all characters with the same rhythmic sense. The solution to this common problem is to develop an awareness to the rhythmic differences of the characters of the play. J. L. Styan states,

> When dramatic impressions follow one another in a related sequence, a new quality arises because they must follow one another at a certain speed in time. We call this new quality 'tempo.' It is a quality every dramatist is anxious to command, because it affects the rhythm of his play and enhances its effect.[17]

Two excellent examples of rhythm and tempo are found in Shakespeare's *Macbeth* and Oscar Wilde's *The Importance of Being Earnest*. The frenzied rhythm of the former is first evident in Act II, Scene iii, and it builds steadily until the end of that scene.

MACDUFF: Awake, awake!
Ring the alarum bell. Murder and treason!
Banquo and Donaldbain! Malcolm! Awake!
Shake off this downy sleep, death's counterfeit,
And look on death itself! Up, up, and see
The great doom's image. Malcolm! Banquo!
As from your graves rise up, and walk like sprites,
To countenance this horror. Ring the bell.

LADY MACBETH: What's the business
That such a hideous trumpet calls to parley
The sleepers of the house? Speak, speak!

MACDUFF: O gentle lady,
'Tis not for you to hear what I can speak.
The repetition, in a woman's ear,
Would murder as it fell.
O Banquo, Banquo!
Our royal master's murdered.

(The scene continues to build its rhythm in smaller climaxes. Actions as well as words further the pace and rhythm.)

MACDUFF: Your royalfather's murdered.

MALCOLM: Oh by whom?

LENNOX: Those of his chamber, as it seemed, had done't.
Their hands and faces were all badged with blood,
So were their daggers, which unwiped we found
Upon their pillows.
They stared, and were distracted, no man's life
Was to be trusted with them.

MACBETH: Oh, yet I do repent me of my fury,
That I did kill them.

MACDUFF: Wherefore did you so?

MACBETH: Who can be wise, amazed, temperate and furious,
Loyal and neutral, in a moment? No man.
The expedition of my violent love
Outrun the pauses reason. Here lay Duncan,
His silver skin laced with his golden blood,
And his gashed stabs looked like a breach in nature
For ruin's wasteful entrance. There, the murderers,
Steeped in the colors of their trade, their daggers
Unmannerly breeched with gore. Who could refrain
That had a heart to love, and in that heart
Courage to make's love known?

LADY MACBETH: Help me hence, ho![18]

The comic rhythm in *The Importance of Being Earnest* builds
slowly but steadily. The rhythm prepares the audience for the ensu-
ing argument which is about to take place between Cecily and
Gwendolyn.

CECILY: Pray let me introduce myself to you. My name is Cecily
Cardew.

GWENDOLYN: Cecily Cardew? What a very sweet name! Something
tells me that we are going to be great friends. I like you already more
than I can say. My first impressions of people are never wrong.

CECILY: How nice of you to like me so much after we have known each
other such a comparatively short time. Pray sit down.

GWENDOLYN: I may call you Cecily, may I not?

CECILY: With pleasure!

GWENDOLYN: And you will always call me Gwendolyn, won't you?

CECILY: If you wish.

GWENDOLYN: Then that is all quite settled, is it not?

CECILY: I hope so.

GWENDOLYN: Perhaps this might be a favorable opportunity for my mentioning who I am. My father is Lord Bracknell. You have never heard of papa, I suppose?

CECILY: I don't think so.

GWENDOLYN: Outside the family circle, papa, I am glad to say, is entirely unknown. I think that is quite as it should be. The home seems to me to be the proper sphere for the man. Cecily, mamma, whose views on education are remarkably strict, has brought me up to be extremely short-sighted. It's part of the system, so you do not mind my looking at you through my glasses?

CECILY: Oh, not at all, Gwendolyn. I am very fond of being looked at.

GWENDOLYN: You are here on a short visit, I suppose.

CECILY: Oh, no! I live here.

GWENDOLYN: Really? Your mother, no doubt, or some female relative of advanced years, resides here also?

CECILY: Oh, no! I have no mother, nor, in fact, any relations.

GWENDOLYN: Indeed?

CECILY: My dear guardian, with the assistance of Miss Prism, has the arduous task of looking after me.

GWENDOLYN: Your guardian?

CECILY: Yes, I am Mr. Worthing's ward.

GWENDOLYN: Oh! It is strange he never mentioned to me that he had a ward. How secretive of him. He grows more interesting hourly. I am not sure, however, that the news inspires me with feelings of unmixed delight. I am very fond of you, Cecily; I have liked you ever since I met you! But I am bound to state that now that I know that you are Mr. Worthing's ward, I cannot help expressing a wish you were—well, just a little older than you seem to be—and not quite so very alluring in appearance. In fact, If I may speak candidly—

CECILY: Pray do! I think that whenever one has anything unpleasant to say, one should always be quite candid.

GWENDOLYN: Well, to speak with perfect candor, Cecily, I wish that you were fully forty-two—and more than usually plain for your age. Ernest has a strong upright nature. He is the very soul of truth and honor. But even men of the noblest possible moral character are extremely susceptible to the influence of the physical charms of others. . . .

CECILY: I beg your pardon, Gwendolyn, did you say Ernest?

GWENDOLYN: Yes.

CECILY: Oh, but it is not Mr. Ernest Worthing who is my guardian. It is his brother—his elder brother.

GWENDOLYN: Ernest never mentioned to me that he had a brother.

CECILY: I am sorry to say they have not been on good terms for a long time.

GWENDOLYN: Ah! that accounts for it. And now that I think of it I have never heard any man mention his brother. The subject seems distasteful to most men.... Of course you are quite, quite sure that it is not Mr. Ernest Worthing who is your guardian?

CECILY: Quite sure. In fact, I am going to be his.

GWENDOLYN: I beg your pardon?

CECILY: Dearest Gwendolyn, there is no reason why I should make a secret of it to you. Our little country newspaper is sure to chronicle the fact next week. Mr. Ernest Worthing and I are engaged to be married.

GWENDOLYN: My darling Cecily, I think there must be some slight error. Mr. Ernest Worthing is engaged to me. The announcement will appear in the *Morning Post* on Saturday at the latest.

CECILY: I am afraid you must be under some misconception. Ernest proposed to me exactly ten minutes ago.

GWENDOLYN: It is certainly very curious, for he asked me to be his wife yesterday afternoon at five-thirty. If you would care to verify the incident, pray do so, I never travel without my diary.... I am so sorry, dear Cecily, if it is any disappointment to you, but I am afraid I have the prior claim.

CECILY: It would distress me more than I can tell you, dear Gwendolyn, if it caused you any mental or physical anguish, but I feel bound to point out that since Ernest proposed to you he clearly has changed his mind.

GWENDOLYN: If the poor fellow has been entrapped into any foolish promise I shall consider it my duty to rescue him at once, and with a firm hand.

CECILY: Whatever unfortunate entanglement my dear boy may have got into, I will never reproach him with it after we are married.

GWENDOLYN: Do you allude to me, Miss Cardew, as an entanglement? You are presumptuous. On an occasion of this kind, it becomes more than a moral duty to speak one's mind. It becomes a pleasure.

CECILY: Do you suggest, Miss Fairfax, that I entrapped Ernest into an engagement? How dare you? This is no time for wearing the shallow mask of manners. When I see a *spade* I call it a *spade*.[19]

Cecily and Gwendolyn pause for a moment to collect their composure. The scene continues to build at a faster pace as each girl slings controlled verbal barbs at the other.

Another effect of rhythmic unawareness occurs when some actors, referred to as "personality actors," conform their character's rhythm to that of their own. While this type of actor may be successful in terms of regularly being cast, he may find after a period of time that he is being typecast, or being given the same types of roles over and over. An often ignored reason for this particular problem lies in the actor's insensitivity to rhythm. He has fallen into an almost inescapable pattern which could be broken by an appreciation for the rhythmic forces which surround him.

> Take a young actor, unformed, undeveloped, but bursting with talent, full of latent possibilities. Quite rapidly he discovers what he can do, and, after mastering his initial difficulties, with a bit of luck he may find himself in the enviable position of having a job which he loves, doing it well while getting paid and admired at the same time. If he is to develop, the next stage must be to go beyond his apparent range, and to begin to explore what really comes hard. But no one has time for this sort of problem. His friends are of little use, his parents are unlikely to know much about his art, and his agent, who may be well-meaning and intelligent, is not there to guide him past good offers of good parts towards a vague something else that would be even better. Building a career and artistic development do not necessarily go hand in hand; often the actor, as his career grows, begins to turn in work that gets more and more similar. It is a wretched story, and all the exceptions blur the truth.[20]

Not only must the actor analyze the rhythm of the play, but he must examine each scene and his role for rhythmic structure. In the process of preparing his role the actor must analyze his own individual responses to rhythm. Are his rhythmic patterns similar to those of the character he seeks to portray, or are they different? Are the visual and auditory rhythms of the character and the actor compatible, or do they conflict and contrast?

Stanislavski recognized the importance of rhythm in performance. "Rhythm is a great thing, but to build up the whole production of a play entirely upon rhythm one must first understand why it is so important."[21] The importance of rhythm lies in its great organizational powers. Through this particular element the actor can create the personality of a dramatic character and contrast it to other characters in the play. The vocal patterns, movements, and emotional makeup of the character become discernible through their rhythmic differences. Life, whether real or as presented on the stage, is organized in the bounds of space through rhythm. Rhythm does not exist in emptiness. Rhythm fills space.

SPACE

Rhythm coexists with the element of space. If you are writing you begin with an empty page. If you are building you begin with an empty site. An empty space must be filled with something— rhythm, movement, color, or silhouette. You must fill your own space in your own way, whether that space is your living environment, your canvas, or your dramatic space.

Space is defined as "the abstract possibility of extension; that which is characterized by limitable dimension; continuous boundless extension in all directions."

Initially, the word space conveys a feeling of vastness, endlessness, and boundlessness, but it can also exist in minuteness. An excellent example of the scope of space can be found in Thornton Wilder's *Our Town*. The character Rebecca illustrates the concept of space from the smallest, seemingly insignificant individual to the interminable vastness of the Mind of God.

REBECCA: I never told you about that letter Jane Crofut got from her minister. . . . The address was like this: It said: "Jane Crofut; The Crofut Farm, Grover's Corners; Sutton County; New Hampshire; United States of America; Continent of North America; Western Hemisphere; the Earth; the Solar System; the Universe; the Mind of God. . . .[22]

Physical spaces vary from the tiny space revealed upon the opening of a matchbox to the closeness of a prison cell to the immensity of the Grand Canyon (see Fig. 3). Most physical spaces are obvious to the individual, for everything exists within the bounds of some kind of space.

Mental spaces also are present in the boundless extension. Concepts, philosophies, ideas and emotions constitute types of mental spaces. In dealing with the intangible components of mental space, one must realize that even the infinite spontaneity of a single fleeting thought exists within space.

Individual responses occur as an awareness to space is developed. The process of self-examination, as in the case of rhythm, plays an important role in the awareness of space. As students of our own self-examination, actors reflect into past experiences to relive certain memories or instances from childhood or adolescence. Through our memories we gain insight into who we are and what we are. Our memories transfer us to the space of our past and from there we may draw upon responses which we can utilize in the creation of a character. Memories can be full of energy and creativity. Time gives us a unique perspective on those moments from the past. With a new perspective, we can use what is valuable and discard what is nonessential.

An actor must develop his ideas concerning space: its color, its texture, its mood and its effect on his overall outlook. As Baker states, "The feelings for space come from where you were born and how you were brought up; whether you were born in the hills or mountains or whether you were born on the plains. I think a lot of your space concept come from the land and from your feelings for it."[23]

Man assesses his feelings for space and seeks to find a means of expressing these sensations. He may exhibit his reactions through the medium of paint, music, movement or, as in the case of the actor, the expressive use of the body and the spoken word.

The actor enjoys great freedom to discover this space and decide how it will be utilized.

> With regard to this element, I think the first essential is that you know you are given freedom to use, for yourself, a large empty space and that what you say in it, what you do in it, and how you use the basic elements which I just demonstrated depend finally on you. How you are going to use the empty space is a prime decision; it is also a great privilege. And it is a joy to know that there is an empty space to work in, in which your imagination can express itself, to know that you can bring yourself to that space and give it an individual expression.[24]

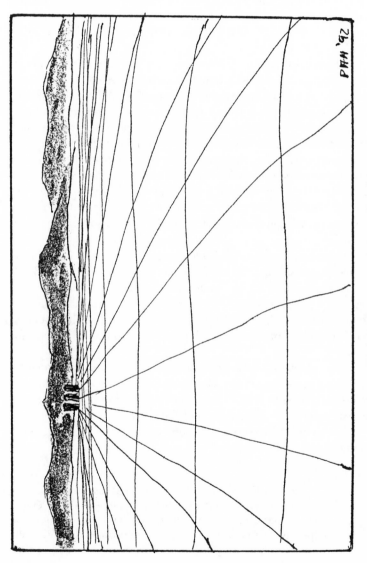

Fig. 3. Visual space (courtesy Patricia Hutchins).

Consider the response to space of the character Laura from Tennessee Williams' *The Glass Menagerie.* Laura is shy, withdrawn and frightened of the outside world and its cruelty, harshness and insensitivity to her. This fear is reflected in her relationship to the space around her. Her life is lived within the context of her family's small apartment and her glass animals. Strangers who enter this guarded space, as in the case of the Gentleman Caller, are admitted reluctantly.

An opposite example of a character's relationship to space is found in Atahuallpa from Peter Shaffer's *The Royal Hunt of the Sun.* Atahuallpa is a king and a god. All of his movements express a control of the space around him. He personifies expansiveness and a oneness with the space he inhabits.

Space is filled through a means of "individual expression" at the discretion of the actor. It is important in work-in-progress in a classroom setting or in the initial stages of rehearsal that the actor work in an empty or blank space. Trappings of other scenes or plays may add unnecessary or distracting factors which will only serve to weaken the actor's concentration and his work. Unlike the dancer, who works primarily with the body, or the visual artist, who chiefly works with line, colors and textures, the actor has at his disposal the body, the voice, and the intellect and the expressive variety accorded each.

SOUND AND SILENCE

Sound and silence are inseparable from space. The various kinds of space are constantly being filled with differing sounds and atmospherically changeable silences.

First in the vast variety of sounds are those classified as nature sounds. Sounds of nature may vary from a powerfully frightening clap of thunder during a storm to the gentle rustle of leaves on a fall day. The sounds of mighty waves crashing against the shore contrast to the sound of spring rain. An excellent illustration of a variety of nature sounds is found in the following excerpt from Walt Whitman's *Song of Myself.*

> Now I will do nothing but listen,
> To accrue what I hear into this song, to let sounds contribute
> toward it.

I hear bravuras of birds, bustle of growing wheat,
Gossip of flames, clack of sticks cooking my meals,
I hear the sounds I love, the sound of the human voice,
I hear all the sounds running together, combined, fused
    of following,
Sounds of the city and sounds out of the city,
    sounds of the day and night,
Talkative young ones to those that like them,
    the loud laugh of work—people at their meals,
The angry base of disjointed friendship, the faint tones of
    the sick,
The judge with hands tight to the desk,
    his pallid-lips pronouncing death-sentence.
The heave'e'yo of stevedores unloading ships by the
    wharves, the refrain of the anchor lifters,
The ring of the alarm-bells, the cry of fire,
    the whirr of swift streaking engines and hose carts with
    premonitory tinkles and color'd lights,
The steam-whistle, the solid roll of the train
    of approaching cars,
The slow march play'd at the head of the association
    marching two and two,
(They go to guard some corpse, the flag-tops are
    draped with black muslin.)
I hear the violincello, ['tis the young man's heart's complaint,]
I hear the key'd cornet, it glides quickly in through my ears,
It shakes mad-sweet pangs through my belly and breast,
I hear the chorus, it is a grand opera,
Ah this indeed is music—this suits me.

A tenor large and fresh as the creation fills me,
The orbic flex of his mouth is pouring and filling me full.

I hear the train'd soprano (what work with hers is this?)
The orchestra whirls me wider that Uranus flies,
It wrenches such ardors from me I did not know
    I possess's them,
It sails me, I dab with bare feet, they are link'd by the
    indolent waves,
I am cut by bitter and angry hail, I lose my breath,
Steep's amid honey'd morphine, my windpipe throttles
    in fakes of death,
At length let up again to feel the puzzle of puzzles,
And that we all Being.[25]

In addition to nature sounds there are mechanical sounds, environmental sounds and human sounds. The most prevalent sample of human sound is of course the voice. Each voice is unique and recognizable because of its specific tone, articulation and quality. Other human sounds include the inhaling and exhaling of breath, the sound of groaning or crying, and the expulsive sound of a sigh.

The following is an exercise which illustrates the emotional impact of the sound of breath and which may be used in class:

Exercise. Have students express the following emotions, states of being or attitudes only through the audible sounds of breathing: boredom, anger, fear, grief, passion and physical pain. Move from student to student and allow each one to express one or all of these examples through breathing. Although students may be exhibiting the same emotion it is amazing how the quality of the sound can differ.

Mechanical sounds include motors, generators and sounds associated with city life. In an effort to make sense of the increasing variety of mechanical sounds, an actor must develop an awareness to sound by returning to the childhood experiences.

Experiments by brain researchers indicate that experiences can be relived through the proper stimuli. In some cases recollections are described more as a reliving than a recalling. It is similar to the *illud tempus*, or "I am there," experience. David Cole identifies the *illud tempus* in *The Theatrical Event* as a sacred presence, or the reality of the existence of a character.

> The remarkable thing about the *illud tempus* is that whereas one might suppose it, of all eras, to have vanished irretrievably, it, in fact, can — unlike the merely historical periods which follow it — be made present again at any moment, by the performance of a ritual. . . .
>
> In a word, the *illud tempus* is not so much *when it first occurred* as *where it is always happening.* And further, since what is always happening is ever-accessible, the *illud tempus* has the potential to be, at any moment, among us.[26]

The idea is similar to the more modern concept of déjà vu or "a distortion or memory in which a new situation or experience is regarded as having happened before." In one such case a woman, while passing a store and hearing music, suddenly felt great sadness and began to weep. Soon after she recalled seeing her mother at the piano playing the same musical piece some forty years before.

This effect corresponds to a particular aspect of the Stanislavski Method of character development. The emotional memory is an exercise in the Method which allows the actor to recall a specific event, sound or feeling from his own past and then associate that response to a similar reaction desired by his character.

> That type of memory which makes you relive the sensations you once felt . . . we call emotion memory. Just as your visual memory can reconstruct an inner image of some forgotten thing, place or person, your emotion memory can bring back feelings you have already experienced. They may seem beyond recall, when suddenly a suggestion, a thought, a familiar object will bring them back in full force. Sometimes the emotions are as strong as ever, sometimes weaker, sometimes the same strong feelings will come back in a somewhat different guise.
>
> [The Director] made the distinction between sensation memory . . . connected with our five senses, and emotion memory. . . . Sight is the most receptive of impressions. Hearing is also extremely sensitive. . . . Although our senses of smell, taste and touch are useful, and even sometimes important . . . their role is merely auxiliary and for the purpose of influencing our emotion memory.
>
> Time is a splendid filter for our remembered feelings— besides . . . it not only purifies, it also transmutes even painfully realistic memories into poetry.
>
> Your first concern should be to find the means of drawing on your emotional material.[27]

By recalling such specific sounds and the reactions to those sounds, the actor can better determine the role sound has played in his life. This discovery is one step on the road to self-awareness.

It is important at this time in the process of self-awareness to consider silence. Silence is obviously the absence of sound, yet silence is altered and modified by emotional content. For example, each of the following silences is void of any sound, yet each is diverse because of the emotional quality, tension, and energy level:

> • The tense silence between the last breath of a dying man and the realization that it was, in fact, his last.
> • The silence of utter aloneness.
> • The electric silence immediately preceding the sinking of the winning putt by a professional golfer.

• The tense, difficult silence that exists between two people who despise one another.
• That silence that rushes in to fill the void after a constant sound ceases.

Silence holds a secret power that makes it a useful tool in the dramatic arts. The actor commands attention and fills the space of the theatre with the application and intermingling of sound and silence. Through an awareness of these related elements the actor is better equipped to recall events of similar consequence and reproduce them on the stage. The actor now has a space in which to perform, a space to fill with rhythms, sounds and dramatic silences.

MOVEMENT

Movement is the essence of life. It carries inner impressions to the outer world and it is our most unique and personal manifestation. When Martha Graham appeared on the Public Broadcasting series *Dance in America* she made the statement, "The body doesn't know how to lie." She was right: the body does not know how to cover up or how to lie about what is going on in the innermost regions of the being. We have become unaccustomed to "reading" the body and we think that body signals or body language have lost their power. Research has suggested that only 7 percent of our responses come from the verbal, 38 percent come from the vocal intonation used in speech, and 55 percent of our reactions to others come from what we see—the visual impression. Movement holds the key to life.

The great dancer and choreographer Doris Humphrey gives further support to the notion of movement as the key to human behavior. "If we understand in our bodies the various ways that force moves and the various sequences that it moves in," she states, "we know something about ourselves because we all as an organism follow the same laws."[28]

Emotions, psychological attitudes and concepts constitute inner movements. These inner movements in turn change and affect the outer movements or those more commonly referred to as body movements or bodily actions.

Human body movements can also be affected by external or

environmental factors. For example, movements are influenced by the type of labor and tensions of one's background. Although attitudes and environmental factors are unique and dissimilar, many times

> underlying all these differences is a fundamental unity, for the word "movement" implies that something is happening. Movement is a universal human characteristic and a person's movement experience begins even before birth. Thus to study movement is to study man, for movement is both the medium and the vehicle for all kinds of human activity and a deeper understanding and a heightened awareness of movement can bring a greater richness to life.[29]

This richness of life achieved through awareness of movement is of prime importance to the modern actor.

Through an awareness of his own movements and movement patterns the actor is better equipped to alter these personal existing patterns to more aptly depict a dramatic character on the stage. Doing so requires cognitive powers of the mind and the sensitivity of the body.

The actor must concern himself with the bodily movements of the character, but he should also study the character's movement through space. How does the character move in the dramatic environment? Are his movements direct, quick and aggressive, or are the movement patterns angular, meandering or plodding? Imagine that your character has paint on the bottoms of his feet and his movements can be traced as he moves throughout the play. What kind of movement patterns will be visible?

Choreographer and dancer Dana Reitz experimented with improvisational techniques that led her to use drawings or mental images and dance movements. She experimented by "drawing her dancing." This improvisational style led her to visually trace the movements of the energy and the flow of movement. Through this approach her dancing movements were recorded as drawing movements (see Fig. 4).

Movements of characters will be affected by a number of variables: costume, time period, style of production, habits, customs and manners of the day, and size of the stage space.

Briefly, movement styles may be described as follows:

Fig. 4. Drawing for the dance *Journey: Moves 1 through 7* (courtesy MIT Press).

• Greek: slow, elegant, stylized, abstracted to express emotion, presentational in form.

• Commedia dell'Arte: somewhat exaggerated and very physical, acrobatic and energetic; rapid, presentational in form.

• Elizabethan: broad and stylized but natural and free flowing; some use of dance, dueling, and acrobatics (the latter for comedy); fluid, presentational in form.

• Neoclassical: elegant, graceful, controlled; much use of hand props, bows, curtsies, and asides; presentational in form.

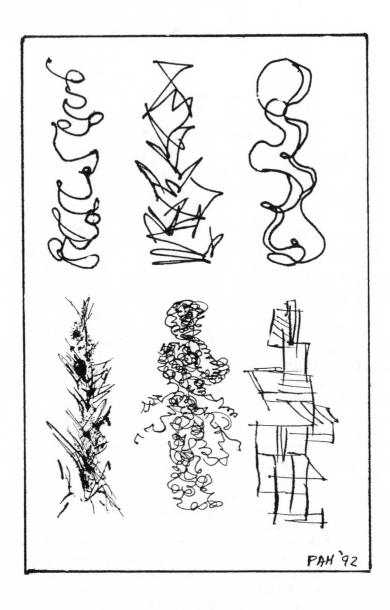

Fig. 5. Examples of abstract movement patterns (courtesy Patricia Hutchins).

• Realistic: actions connected to the character's thoughts, emotions, and speech; highly individualized; representational in form.
  • Non-Realistic (expressionism, surrealism, etc.): some use of distortion; movements may be more connected to symbols or ideas; presentational or representational in form.
  • Post-modern (Theatre of the Absurd): movements may borrow from any or all other styles in combination with ritualistic and/or neuro-linguistic styles.

A sensitive awareness of movement does not mean that the actor should develop his body to the extent of a dancer, but rather that the actor should become sensitive and aware of movement to the degree that it expresses stimuli from the world. Through movement the human form cuts space, forming shapes, masses and lines.

LINE AND DIRECTION

Line is the intangible path cut in space between the beginning and end of a movement. Direction is the course that line pursues. Line is the end product of a specific movement and direction is a component. Line, which can be curved or straight, extends in many directions. The body executes straight movements in the same manner as spokes extend from a wheel. An example of straight movement is a traffic policemen extending his arm to stop oncoming traffic. Curved movements, such as throwing a softball, cut arc-like paths in space. "Directional movement appears as the most basic form in which movement establishes a relationship to the surrounding space."[30]

Along the path man travels en route toward individuality, he becomes aware of the variety of lines in his surroundings. Thoughts, beliefs, specific words, shapes and symbols all present an assortment of lines. One need only imagine the word "evasive" and a meandering, uncertain line is suggested. When one pictures the shape of an octagon a stop sign flashes in the mind's eye.

Line can work much the same way in the actor's conception of a theatrical character. A forceful, extroverted character would execute lines in space which are straight and direct, whereas a shy character would produce light, indefinite directions of lines in moving through space.

Fig. 6. An abstract representation of a character (courtesy Patricia Hutchins).

Assume you were to prepare an abstract line drawing of your character–not a line drawing of how the character moved through space (movement pattern) but an abstraction of the actual character (see Fig. 5 and Fig. 6).

Also consider the line and direction of the character's gestures and mannerisms, posture and body stance. Line and direction reveal overt patterns of the character's inner intention. In essence line and direction provide an objective picture whereby the actor can study and analyze his character's overall movements.

SILHOUETTE

Silhouette is an ingredient of line. As line pursues a direction in space, it forms outlines of shapes which compose silhouette. The silhouette or body image may provide simple details about the character such as height, weight, posture, body stance, body conformity and any physical peculiarities. Silhouette also can point out emotional qualities of the character. Certain postures may connote suppressed rage. Height in relation to other characters may be a telltale sign of dominance. Physical handicaps or peculiarities may signify deeper emotional conflicts.

The body creates silhouette and shapes in space through movement. The creation of silhouette or shaping is illustrated in the following:

> Shaping is the aspect of movement form which allows the mover to accommodate to the plastic character of objects in space, to their volume, or contour, their three dimensionality, and consequently to mold space into plastic forms himself, whether in clay as the sculptor does, or in thin air as the dancer, mime and storyteller do. In shaping, the active part of the body constantly adapts to the forms of space. . . .[31]

Silhouette can work much the same way in the actor's conception of a theatrical character as line does. A proud character's body silhouette would likely be composed of straight, direct, and tall lines. A weak and downtrodden character's lines would struggle and strive for mere existence.

The element of silhouette may seem more directly relevant to the work of the visual or graphic artist, but the director is often

Top: Fig. 7. *Bottom:* Fig. 8. Silhouette samples (courtesy Patricia Hutchins).

concerned with silhouette as it contributes to the total stage picture — one made of three dimensional actors against a two or three dimensional set. The actor should make use of the benefits of this element as well. Silhouette provides an "outside-in" perspective of the character for the actor, helping him to visualize the character and his relation to others on the stage. Silhouette is powerful in the simplicity to which images are reduced (see Fig. 7 and Fig. 8).

TEXTURE AND COLOR

Humans unconsciously characterize things according to texture and color. Both elements are perceived visually, and texture is also perceived as a tactile stimulus. Humans not only see color and texture but experience them emotionally — green envy, red anger or blue mood. Furthermore, textural reactions are conjured up by such specific personality traits as gruffness, sluggishness, sophistication and hypertension.

Texture applies to movement as well as to voice quality. Texture and color are important design elements as both are represented in the set design, lighting, costumes, props and furnishings of the play.

These two elements seldom exist in and of themselves. Texture and color are inherent qualities which coexist in the presence of any or all of the preceding elements mentioned in this chapter (see Fig. 9).

We are granted the intellectual facilities with which to rise above other forms of life and express unique responses to experiences. The actor who seeks to be called a creative artist employs his awareness of life and through these elements (rhythm, space, sound and silence, movement, line and direction, silhouette, and texture and color) projects into a world of patterns some undeniably unique spark.

This creative philosophy provides the actor with a means of defining certain factors present in his life and analyzing his reactions to and perceptions of those factors. His experiences give the actor the material through which he is capable of creating something singularly rare. These experiences, classified according to the elements, coupled with the energy and the desire for a means of individual expression, are the tools necessary for the abilities inherent in every person to become integrated. The individual needs only

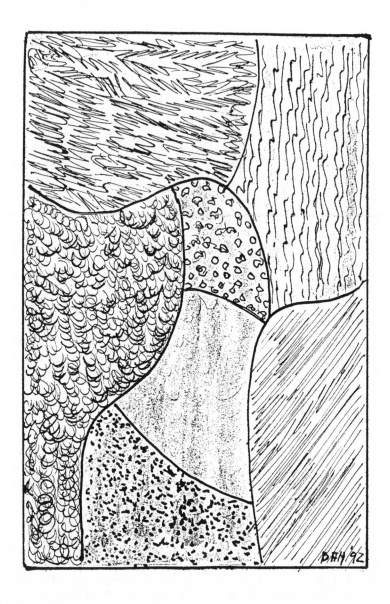

Fig. 9. Visual texture (courtesy Patricia Hutchins).

motivation, imagination and confidence in the existence of his creative talents to become a truly creative individual.

INTEGRATION VS. STANISLAVSKI'S SYSTEM

Contemporary theatre practitioners owe a debt to Stanislavski each time they study, rehearse and perform a role.

> Whether we laud or condemn Stanislavski's theories on stage performance, what we must accept is that at the center of the discussion of this man and his work there exists a wealth of information on the subject of actors and actor training. To dismiss this information is to turn our backs on what is certainly the most influential force in the theatre world of the twentieth century.[32]

Stanislavski asked the actor to explore the outer, or physical life of the role and the inner, or psychological life of the role. Stanislavski said,

> The creation of the physical life is half the work on a role because, like us, a role has two natures, physical and spiritual. To permeate external physical actions with inner essentials, the spiritual life of a part, you must have appropriate material. This you find in the play and in your role ... because a role, more than action in real life, must bring together the two lives — of external and internal action — in mutual effort to achieve a given purpose.[33]

Paul Baker's integration of abilities plan also asks the actor to look at all aspects of the role: the spiritual, the physical, the intellectual, the emotional/psychological and the all important connection between the role and the actor's inner and outer life.

Baker says in reference to the rhythm of a character,

> In this [exercise] you begin with an object and work from that to adjectives to rhythm to a live human being ... Once you get a rhythm you can begin to develop a character. The key to it is that you develop your character honestly from those descriptive words and from those rhythms. Don't work them around to produce what you would like them to be ... Don't merge them or

blend them or lessen them to make the character easier to perform. You have to learn the value of contradictions, of opposites
which build tensions. It is basic to drama . . . Your character
may be very strange, very unusual. You may come up with something really brilliant in this case. Many of you will. Some
characters you have never seen or heard of before. Don't let
yourself go back and belittle the character and force him into
some little cut and dried preconceived concept. Let's try to
bring a fresh character out of this.[34]

Both Baker and Stanislavski have recognized the valuable element of rhythm. Stanislavski based the entire production on a
rhythmic unity that pervaded the play. Baker stresses that the
essence of character is in rhythm.

Stanislavski suggests to the actor that making a list of physical
actions is important. The actor should have an understanding of the
physical actions of the character and work those actions or other
types of action which the playwright has established into the play.
This "list" style of studying a role is a technique Stanislavski used
with his actors and one that Baker suggests in the initial encounter
with the character. The word study of the Ten Line Exercise sets the
actor on his way in a positive direction in the initial stages of
character study. Words, phrases and images are important to establish before continuing to more advanced stages of character work.

Both Baker and Stanislavski appreciate the value of muscle
memory. Stanislavski based much of his theories of the *method of
physical actions* on the basic kinesthetic fact of muscle memory.

With time and frequent repetition, in rehearsal and performance, this score becomes habitual. An actor becomes so accustomed to all his objectives and their sequence that he cannot
conceive of approaching his role otherwise than along the lines
of the steps fixed in the score. Habit plays a great part in
creativeness: it establishes in a firm way the accomplishments of
creativeness. . . . Habit creates second nature, which is a second
reality. The score automatically stirs the actor to physical
action.[35]

The score of which Stanislavski speaks is the *method of physical
actions.*

Baker acknowledges the value and use of muscle memory. He

suggests that we lose our ability to respond to muscle memory through age, rigid thinking and a loss of acceptance of our own creative uniqueness.

> . . . We want you to rediscover the pleasure of working with your muscles.
> The premise is that your muscles are fairly honest. And what we're going to do is based on your listening to the way your muscular reactions speak to you. It is based on your going back and recapturing that joy of movement. It is based on recapturing the joy of throwing a ball, the joy of catching one, the joy of physical movement through space. . . . This is a very basic thing . . . . We want to go back and wake up your reaction to physical movement.[36]

Stanislavski demanded that the actor train himself as a "whole instrument." The mind-body connection was an important element in the creation of any role. Baker too emphasizes the "whole instrument" idea but with the Greek point of view.

The Greeks believed in an organic knowledge of self. Their belief in the attainment of a higher ideal set by a standard which was socially acceptable is similar to the goals established by Baker's integration of abilities. You learn by doing. You learn by connection. You learn by accepting that you are a part of a greater whole. You learn by relating your experiences with space and sound and rhythm to other elements in your creative work.

The choice study portion of the Ten Line Exercise encourages the actor to investigate any aspect of the play, the playwright's life, the character or special actions performed by the character which need further work. This may involve research, foreign language work, accent work, dance work, or a re-examination of movement, sound or rhythmic aspects of the character.

Stanislavski also encouraged such exploration for a full understanding of the character within the context of the play.

> A real artist must lead a full, interesting, varied and exciting life. He should know not only what is going on in the big cities, but in the provincial towns, faraway villages, factories and the big cultural centres of the world as well. He should study the life and psychology of the people who surround him, of various other parts of the population, both at home and abroad.

We need a broad point of view to act the plays of our times and of many peoples. . . . To reach the pinnacle of fame an actor has to have more than his artistic talents, he must be an ideal human being . . . capable of reaching the high points of his epoch, of grasping the value of culture in the life of his people, . . . of reflecting the spiritual cravings of his contemporaries.[37]

The integration of abilities makes use of many theories and methods of actor training as well as creative thought. Paul Baker certainly has been influenced by Stanislavski, but also by the works of Frank Lloyd Wright, the Bauhaus Group and visual artists such as Picasso, Mondrian, Rouault and Klee.

The integration of abilities is a unique approach to creative work because it synthesizes many points of view and because it does not reject the theories of any who strive for integrity, honesty and creative growth. Methodologies in science, art, theatre, music, dance, design and problem solving take their place in the integration of abilities. Stanislavski was not limited by his access to these methodologies. He was bound by the times in which he lived. If he were alive today it is certain that he and Paul Baker would have much to share.

Every actor should explore similar questions about his role. He should find the questions in the play and solve them for himself with identification. Whether he uses real or imaginary experiences, or both, is unimportant as long as he can believe in them and tap them when he needs them.

— UTA HAGEN

III

EXERCISES FOR CREATIVE GROWTH

According to noted psychologist Abraham Maslow, creative people "are self-actualized persons, not dissimilar to those who undergo 'peak performance.' These are profound and invasive moments of life that change the person and his appreciation of the world...."[38]

The exercises outlined in this chapter are designed to promote the natural creativity which the actor must draw upon in the creation of his character. These exercises do not provide a quick fix or an easy solution to a character problem or block which may inhibit or restrict the actor and his work. What they do provide are creative options for the actor. The actor must personalize the character and make it his own with his unique approach and personification. Many actors just do what works, or what comes easily or quickly, or what has proved successful in the past.

Perhaps they do so out of necessity since few directors have the time (or take the time) to offer assistance and help. They are concerned with getting the show on stage within the budget. They may not have the time to coach, teach or cajole an inexperienced actor into his character. Some actors may take the easy way out because of fear. Auditioning for a role can be a terrifying experience.

The exhilaration and excitement may soon give way to feelings of fear and inadequacy, especially if the role is particularly demanding or different from the actor's own experience or personality. It is easy to see why so many actors resort to using techniques which are familiar and safe. But each time an actor begins work on a character he asks the same questions: Where do I begin? How do I start this process of characterization? What if the "old ways" don't provide me with what I need to explore this character?

Ultimately the actor can only begin with himself—his motivation, effort, experience and intellect, and a faith in his ability. The actor must trust himself. He must say no to "cookie cutter" acting, no to acting like he has in the past, and no to acting like someone else has acted in the past. Each character is a new character. Every performance is unlike any performed before.

The process of acting should not be a mystery, yet it often is difficult to describe or apply. Too many times I have witnessed student actors (usually inexperienced ones who are eager just to be on stage) who think that acting involves only learning lines and the blocking. They spend most of their time memorizing. This is a small but necessary part of the process and it is far from the total craft of acting.

Mind and body must come together with the idea of the character as presented by the playwright, as adapted by the director, and as fits into a contemporary social context. Then and only then is a unified performance realized. Acting as art or craft should be approached with the same work effort that dancers and visual artists use in the development of their art or craft.

Much of the actor's work is mental and intellectual, like that of a detective or psychiatrist. The actor is always looking for clues from the play, the director, the things other characters say about his character and his own experiences. Like the psychiatrist, the actor in search of insight into the character analyzes, judges and speculates on the whys and hows of his character's actions, thoughts and words.

Silvano Arieti outlines six conditions of creative thinking which can be applied directly to the actor and his creative work.

First is receptivity. The actor must be open to the ideas or images which may present themselves as part of the creative work. We cannot always use brute force to push for ideas, but an open or accepting attitude will sometimes allow for clear thinking, and the solution may present itself unexpectedly.

An important aspect of receptivity is concentration, or, to use a word I prefer, focusing. The actor must focus on the work at hand and not allow outside distractions to become so prominent that the work is jeopardized. Focusing is especially important in rehearsal for a play or for work in progress in class. Often the actor is so preoccupied with how he is progressing or what others may think of his work that he becomes inhibited and ultimately opts for the quick fix.

Focusing sharpens the actor's abilities so that he may work on one specific aspect of the character at a time instead of approaching the entire play. In the early stage receptivity allows the actor the freedom to play, to invent and to experiment without the worry or confinement of a particular result. This step is important since acting is a journey and not a destination. The actor is continually working to perfect his work.

The second condition is immersion. Through focusing the actor can immerse himself in the process of character work. This might involve, for example, studying a particular period of history for a period play. It can also mean that the actor might explore a certain physical or vocal technique inherent in the character such as fencing for Restoration dramas, dancing for Shakespearean plays or musical comedies, or a physical disability like that needed in a performance of *The Elephant Man.*

Vocal work might be needed to portray a character with an accent or one with peculiar speech patterns. Immersion in character work will enable the actor to assess the total scope of the performance — how much work is needed and to what extent he will need to study and train.

Third is the ability to see the right questions and the knowledge that one has permission to fail. Sometimes in the process of working on a character the actor will come to a question with no clear answer. Why does the character say this? Why does he do this or that? What is the character thinking or feeling at this particular moment? Reconstruct the question: Why does the character *not* say this? Why does he *not* do this or that? If asking the question in another way does not provide some clues, make up an answer that you can use to associate yourself with the character's actions or words.

This manner of questioning reveals another way of thinking and of questioning the character: Don't overlook the obvious or the trivial. Don't be afraid to fail. One of the things my acting teacher used to say at the beginning of each class was "Don't be afraid to get egg on your face." You will probably know when you have made a mistake; if not, the director, teacher or other actors will surely let you know. The important thing is not to be afraid to try, to experiment, and if necessary to fail. People may laugh or you might get a bad review, but you are learning, growing and becoming.

The fourth condition is fluency of thinking. For the actor this means an abundance of ideas. Flood your mind with associations, words, images and insights into the character. Draw upon your own experimental associations and words. Much of this work will be discarded by the time of the last performance but it is important to have a richness from which to draw initial thinking.

Fifth is flexibility, a condition that corresponds to the permission to fail. Sometimes what seems was a perfectly good idea just doesn't work out. Be flexible so you can abandon the old ways and make room for a new idea or approach. Be flexible so you can be receptive.

Sixth is originality. Each actor can bring something unique to each performance. We all lead different lives offstage and consequently we bring that difference to the characters onstage. Don't restrict that natural originality; instead empower yourself with it.

Another aspect of originality in performance is what I call "the illusion of the first time." The actor should approach each performance with an appreciation for the originality inherent in it. After all, the audience is different, the cast may be different, and you the actor are different in some way.

Imagine playing eight performances a week on Broadway or in some regional theatre. How can you make each performance alive and fresh? How can you keep yourself from becoming complacent or bored? Remind yourself of the originality of the moment. You are performing in *this* play in *this* theatre on *this* day. You may have played Blanche from *A Streetcar Named Desire* many times in other theatres with other casts but this performance will be unique. This is the major difference between film acting and stage acting. Film is the same time and time again. No stage performance will ever be exactly duplicated.

These six conditions should serve as a constant reminder for the actor. Your ways of thinking about acting and your attitude toward the process of acting should be flexible and from a strong position of artistic integrity.

The Ten Line Exercise: The Six Studies

The Ten Line Exercise is a series of six studies which are designed to promote the creative growth of the actor in his work in progress. The first five studies culminate in a final study called the ten line study. This final step should be approached after all of the previous studies are completed or as the actor feels comfortable in moving on to the next step.

The first five studies — the word study, the sound study, the visual study, the movement study and the choice study — are presented in an order which can be most useful, but the order of these five studies may be changed as necessary.

These studies are provided for the professional actor, the student actor or the actor in non-professional theatres. They are for actors working on roles for auditions or for performance. These studies are useful for any actor working alone without the benefit of director, teacher, coach or classmate.

The Ten Line Exercise began as a necessary evil and is a solution to a number of problems which actors often face both in their training and in production of various plays.

Among the many problems facing student actors is the lack of rehearsal time for assignments. This problem is similar to the lack of individual attention given actors while in rehearsal. Most acting classes solve this problem by assigning scenes to students, but this often means the students are only able to do that particular scene.

Professional as well as student actors encounter the same problems in their initial character development and early rehearsal periods. These studies were formulated in part to relieve these particular problems and still allow for the creative growth of the individual. Sally Netzel, formerly of the Dallas Theatre Center and currently a writer/actress, states:

> [The exercises] do not substitute for skill, inherent ability or work. It provides a vocabulary and method to integrate the elements.... [These exercises] are especially beneficial to the

American actor who often lacks formal training and tends to depend entirely too much on emotion as a tool in acting.[39]

Professional, non-professional and student actors may face a number of different problems in working on a character. Fellow actors or the director may be incompatible or difficult to work with. (Jealousy and in-fighting are not uncommon on the stage or film set.) Further, not all directors are skilled or experienced, and the directions they provide may be inadequate or misguided. Finally, the director may take little or no time with the actor.

The actor has little choice but to create the character on his own. The director will most likely provide critical comments at a later time—usually close to final rehearsal or performance. Few directors are allowed the time to conduct class during rehearsal or to offer helpful instructions as the actor works on the character. The actual work on a character is "home" work—that is, to be conducted by the actor outside the rehearsal studio. Away from the stage or set the actor can utilize the Ten Line Exercise in his individual work on the character.

These studies are sufficiently flexible to allow individual students to explore qualities inherent in themselves and discover a means through which they could best work. They permit a long period of development; in fact they could cover a full semester of work in a classroom situation to diminish the desire for a quick result characterization. They anticipate the possible circumstance in which a director, through lack of time or desire, cannot work out with the actor a means of investigating the character. They suggest a means of developing a proper, in-depth personality for a major or minor role. They make use of the time the actor spends working alone to help the actor find his inner dialogue with himself and discover his own uniqueness.

These studies are steps of parts of a total process which is an exercise. An exercise is executed to explore, to stretch and to strengthen. This exercise is a means to an end, not an end in itself. If these studies are performed as part of a classroom situation their effectiveness should not be judged on the pass/fail basis of ordinary grading systems, but rather with the attitude of expressing exactly what was communicated by the actor. The audience (in this case the classmates and instructor) should be concerned with the following questions which measure the effectiveness of the work in progress:

What was communicated?

What was the quality of the work in progress?*

Was the actor connected to the character in action or in words?

Did the work in progress have a feeling of unity and a sense of wholeness to it?

What are the overall impressions of the work in progress?

What, if any, personal associations do you have with this work?

Classmates or instructors should be as specific as possible in offering feedback on the work in progress. Images, words or word phrases can be used to explain what was communicated by the student actor.

The Word Study

The actor should compile a word list or word group for the chosen character. The word study should be updated upon subsequent readings of the play. This list is composed of impressions and images gained in the readings of the play. The words may include phrases and associations that the actor has about the character or himself playing the character. No attempt should be made to work these word lists or groups into sentences or paragraphs. As Sally Netzel explains, "Many actors are word or literarily inclined. This initial step in character development takes advantage of that inclination without narrowing the initial concepts into any particular form. The word 'list' does not imply a form, i.e. rows of words."[40]

The list might include likes and dislikes of the character or perhaps objects, sounds, colors, textures or attitudes of the character and his environment. The study encourages the actor to use adjectives and attitudes the character has toward other factors in the play. For example, in preparation of the character Linda Loman from Arthur Miller's *Death of a Salesman,* the actor might include household articles, sounds, smells and chores associated with the kitchen. Since the character is a housewife these factors would definitely affect the personality of the character and therefore should be noted. The word study helps the actor explore facets of the life of the character which are not necessarily presented on the stage.

---

*Work in progress is a more appropriate term than performance since the student actor is investigating the character in various stages of work in progress.

By living or exploring the character's "offstage" life the actor can develop a broader and more enriched character on the stage. This is especially beneficial for the actor working on a role with few lines or little time on stage. He is able to make an insignificant character significant.

In effect, the word study is a record of the words or word phrases which answer a variety of questions the actor might put to his character. It is important not to intellectualize these words and images but rather to note any that come to mind.

The practice of questioning the character and noting impressions is supported in the writings of Michael Chekhov.

> By working this way you will be able to study and create your character more profoundly (and more quickly, too): You will not be relying only on ordinary thinking instead of "seeing" these little "performances." Dry reasoning kills your imagination. The more you probe with your analytical mind, the more silent becomes your feelings, the weaker your will and the poorer your chances for inspiration.[41]

The actor should keep the word list as a reference throughout the development of the character and during rehearsal. Some associations will not be used in the later stages of work, but others may become extremely important — they may, in fact, touch the very essence of the character.

If the word study is conducted as part of a class or as an exercise used in the rehearsal of a play for performance, actors may share their notes and ask for feedback. It is important to note that the word study is a personal exercise and efforts should be made to avoid injecting ideas from other actors. Other actors' notions of the character could prove stifling for the actor at work in these preliminary stages of character development.

Part of Paul Baker's integration of abilities exercises involves writing associations and responses to a nature object or other inanimate object. Baker suggests writing about the color, the texture, the line and the mass of the object. Students should try to identify the rhythm and spatial character of the object. In essence, get to know your object from a sensory point of view. This will help you develop a character from the responses you have to the object.

I have performed this exercise, as have many of my students.

Sometimes students chose a rock, a piece of bone, a piece of wood, a shell or a leaf. It is best to choose an object you can handle rather than something so large that it would be difficult to move it and examine it from many points of view.

Baker suggests that students approach the object at different times of the day, in different moods and with different outlooks. For example, look at the object when you are tired, when you are sick, when you awaken and when you are hungry. What does it remind you of? What are its lines suggestive of? Does it have a particular smell? What are the predominant colors? Be careful not to think too literally and not to rush your responses or go for what you think will work easily.

Be open to where your creative imagination will take you. Be ready to be amazed at what your creativity can offer. Baker warns that this is not easy. It is an exercise that can take you headlong into your own means of resistance, your own creative barriers and your own desire for the quick fix. Remind yourself that this is a process. In this exercise the journey is more important than the destination.

The nature object exercise leads the way to more advanced creative work. It establishes a sense of honesty within the actor as he approaches his work. It gives him courage and faith in the journey.

Following the nature object exercise is the rhythm study, and finally the character emerges.

The explanations lie dormant deep inside of us, in our subconscious, in our emotions. When we say we will be honest about a piece of work, we are proposing a very complicated process. It begins long before we ever do anything on stage.

Write down everything that crosses your mind. You may start to work on a certain problem and write pages and pages. Then go back and relate the pattern or patterns of these reactions to your previous ones. You begin to find there is a similarity between them, very little freshness there. The patterns have been borrowed or adopted from many different sources. None of them really belong to you. Honesty is trying to find who you are and what you are. Let that thought communicate through your projection of the exercise; let it distill through you. . . .

It takes a lot of strength to genuinely face up to the material you are producing and to say to yourself that this is fresh and new and the rest is borrowed. If you get a few seconds of fresh good work, that is enough to build a whole edifice on. Honesty comes through having enough dialogue with oneself to recognize established patterns, patterns that are worn and imitative, that come from the outside and are result-oriented. Honesty about yourself might help you go inside and find fresh reactions.[42]

The Sound Study

The actor should construct a sound study of the chosen character, avoiding any use of dialogue and considering vocal sounds, intonations, environmental sounds and sounds which evoke mental images. For example, the character of Linda in *Death of a Salesman* might evoke sounds of the kitchen — chopping food, boiling water, the clamor of pots and pans — while at the same time the actor might express various attitudes of the character and her personality. The actor could perhaps express the maternal contentedness of Linda in the opening of the play through humming or quietly singing. The final lonely futility of the character could be portrayed through the audible vocalization of a single vowel.

Other characters with varying experiences would, of course, require a different kind of sound, either mental or environmental. The actor may wish to use certain musical scores to convey specific feelings or emotions, but it is wise to keep the use of musical compositions to a minimum. The wide range of emotional responses any piece can evoke can reduce the control often necessary in actor communication.

The purpose of the sound study is to expand the actor's knowledge of the character's audible traits and rhythms and, more important, to explore sound in both abstract and real senses of communication. The actor may discover personal reactions to sounds which are similar to or different from those of the character. In this study the actor should apply these personal reactions to specific sounds in order to achieve a desired response, corresponding to the Stanislavski emotion memory exercise.

The actor may utilize a tape recorder, demonstrate the exercise live, or use both means of communicating the sound exercise. If this study is conducted as part of a class or rehearsal session, the results rely greatly upon the responses of the classmates or other members of the cast.

As the sound study is performed, other students note responses on paper in stream of consciousness writing. After the completion of the performance, the words noted are read to the performer. Although there is always some variance in individual responses because of individual background and experience, it becomes clear what sounds communicated part or all of the character. A discussion follows that should lead the performer into ideas of actual usable sounds that might be used in a performance of the character. Often, this results in ideas of a technical nature such as voice quality, footstep rhythm, etc. The discussion may also point out abstract senses or feelings that may later be incorporated into a performance. Again, no judgments are made, so no right or wrong way is implied.[43]

The sound study gives the actor an opportunity to increase his awareness of the auditory factors useful in performing his character. The actor, in effect, creates a "soundtrack" of the character. Sound may be more important to one character than to another, but nonetheless sound plays an integral role in the life of any character.

The Visual Study

Some actors are verbal or literary. Some may relate more to sound or music. Still other actors may express themselves best through a visual means. The visual study helps the actor to visually conceptualize the character. The character may be expressed visually through any medium that epitomizes the character, whether it be sculpture, collage, a painting, a textural composition, or a nature object such as a rock, piece of wood, or leaf. An abstract painting could be used to express the character or an object from the actor's personal life which, when visualized, evokes a desired response.

The effectiveness of the visual study, like the sound study, relies upon the responses of the classmates and instructor, or the members of the cast and the director. The visual studies are examined by members of the class or cast and their reactions, attitudes and conclusions are in turn reported to the actor. It is actually more effective and more interesting if each member of the class or cast displays his or her visual work without the others' knowing which study pertains to which character. This grants greater honesty in class reactions.

The actor working alone on the visual study can explore the

character through visual means in terms of color, texture, design, etc. Motifs, shapes, colors and textures can be most helpful in connecting the actor with his role.

The actor working alone may have additional time to ponder and analyze the visual study—live with the visual study, so to speak, and therefore benefit from what may have been unconscious visual responses to the character or the physical aspects of the play or the character.

The purpose of this study is to state visually certain factors inherent in the character which the actor may have already discovered through the word or sound study. This study is more concrete and tangible than the other studies and therefore allows for unique contributions made in the area of design and composition.

The Movement Study

Movement affords the actor a unique and important medium through which to explore and express his character. Since all characters move in some way, movement is essential to character portrayal.

> All manner of performance involves distinctive actions and draws its character from body movement patterns, but the role of movement in performance can be so taken for granted that it is easily ignored. Analysis of expressive movement in performance promises discovery, not trivial observation. Movement has direct impact in the emotional-interactional contexts in which we participate with spoken words more properly seen as modifiers, dependent for their meaning on the patterns sound and movement delineate in our day-to-day performance.[44]

The actor must be able to analyze the character's facial expressions, mannerisms, movements (sitting, walking, gesturing, handling objects) and overall movement patterns.

The actor must be able not only to assess the character's movements but also to connect those movements to an inner thought, feeling or motivation. Characters in a play often move unconsciously just as real people do. The actor, however, can never move unconsciously as the character. He must know how and why and when he is moving as he is.

The movement study is a character study expressed in movements, abstract or real, which depicts the personality and life of the character. The study should not be approached as a choreographed dance or dance piece of any kind. On the contrary, the study is an investigative composition of the mental, physical and emotional qualities of the character as expressed through movement. Dance may play an important role in the study of some characters, but this study should not be looked at as a dance exercise in which the actor choreographs his movements. Dance background can be very helpful in plays in which characters are called upon to move in a stylized fashion, such as classical Greek tragedies. Many plays from Shakespeare to Molière call on characters to perform period dance or court dance sequences. The character Nora in Ibsen's *A Doll's House* dances the tarantella, and many musical comedy roles require dancing as part of the *corps de danse* or have solo sequences.

Daily movements may be included as part of the movement study. These would include sewing, eating and drinking, smoking, personal grooming habits, playing card games, and many other types of movements that the character would perform in the play.

Abstract movement can best express a character's emotional or inner self. If the character is involved in a struggle throughout the play, the actor might devote the movement study to analyzing the emotional qualities of struggle and the resulting physical responses. The actor could choose to express the character through a series of abstract movements as the play progresses, or the character could be demonstrated through the tensions or flow of a single gesture. A variety of means can be employed, but it is to the advantage of the actor to explore all the possible facets and attitudes of the character through movement.

Since the emphasis is on emotional characteristics as expressed through movement, the use of music, sound and costumes is to be avoided. Rhythms may at one time or another be used, and if the character is historical, appropriate attire may be used.

Movements can constitute the most expressive elements of an actor's role. This in-depth study of the character's inner and outer movement patterns lends greater credibility to the actor's portrayal.

The Choice Study

The choice study is used to explore any aspect of the character which the actor feels needs additional investigation. Any of the preceding studies, with the exception of the word study, may be reproduced with a new and more enlightened point of view.

In the preparation of historical characters the actor may do research on costumes of the period (and their effect on movement), actual history as it relates to the character, or literature of the specific period.

The actor may wish to do research on any interest of the character as indicated by the text of the play. For example, if a specific character is influenced by a certain ideology or philosophy, the actor might study that particular ideology.

The actor might also find it enlightening to do research on the playwright or the style in which the play is written, such as expressionism, theatre of the absurd, or theatre of cruelty. Although such investigation is permissible as intellectual research, it is beneficial to conduct a choice exercise which does more than provide the actor with mere historical facts or trivial information.

Another interesting study that may be carried out in the choice exercise is the placing of oneself in the actual environment of the character to facilitate understanding through experiencing similar events. The actor may also try sustaining the character in the actor's own environment, an exercise which provides an interesting insight into character objectivity.

The choice study might be more appropriately titled "your exercise" for this study is literally the choice of the individual actor. The purpose of this study is to allow the actor a chance to explore aspects of the character or the play as a whole.

This study may be presented in the form of a performance, a study, or an informative discussion/lecture on the pertinent material gained through research or further study by the actor.

The Ten Line Study

At this point the actor should be able to synthesize the insight and information about the character gained by performing the preceding studies. This synthesis is the ten line study.

The actor should select approximately ten lines from the play which he feels display a variety of emotional levels and facets of the character and demonstrate the progression of the character during the play. These lines should, in most cases, be left in chronological order so that the proper flow and progression of the character can be maintained. The actor may refer to and use any of the material from any or all of the preceding studies. The ten line study is in effect the performance of the character through the entire play as expressed through roughly ten lines chosen from the play. The transitions from one line to another may be made with the use of abstract movements, sounds, or rhythmic phrases performed vocally or physically.

The "audience" notes the emotions and progressions as communicated by the actor. Although these judgments are virtually a feedback of what was actually communicated, the audience should with this study be more critical in their assessment and comments, since at this point the actor should be ready to duplicate the character on the stage.

The purpose of the ten line study is to provide the actor with a means of pulling all the preceding studies into a final composition which expresses a multifaceted character in a variety of emotional levels.

The actor should at this time be able to perceive the progression he has made from the initial word study through sound, visual and movement studies, and finally to the performance of the character.

Our calling is the art and craft of presenting a personality to an audience.

—LAURENCE OLIVIER

IV

THE ACTOR WORKING ALONE

Every actor is in a sense a student. In approaching every new play or character, the actor, regardless of his level of experience, must prepare to study the intended role, to discover all facets of the character and finally to learn more of the complexities of human nature. The guided instruction given the neophyte is no longer offered as the actor becomes more experienced, so the actor must seek methods of preparing roles which he can utilize while working alone.

Dramatic Analysis

It may seem unnecessary to suggest that actors should read the entire play before beginning any work on it, but I am continually surprised to find that many novice actors fail to read the entire play before beginning their work for an audition or rehearsal. Young and often inexperienced actors enrolled in an acting class may be given an assignment to prepare a monologue or scene, usually from one of the student-actors' scenebooks or workbooks which include a wide variety of two person scenes and monologues from plays and screenplays. They read no further than the two or three pages of the scene reproduced in the book. Short introductions provided by the editors of these scenebooks are helpful, but they by no means provide a complete understanding of the characters and their intentions, the character relationships and the plot line or significance of the play's theme.

Actors should not only read the play but reread it at least three times before beginning any creative work. Read first for content and a sense of flow: Who is who and what are they doing? Read second for more details, especially those which concern your character. Read the third time for answers to your preliminary questions.

Those questions are the who, what, when, where and (most important) why of your character. You should know how you are, what you are doing in the play and in each scene, when the time period and time frame of the play is, and where the play is occurring. Finally, you must know why your character wants whatever he or she wants in the play. Student actors sometimes complain that the play does not provide all that information. Quite true! So make it up, calling on your own creative imagination. Make up what works for you and fits in logically with the context of the play. The playwright may never find it necessary to state that your character was born in Ohio or Florida, but if it is important for you to have that information to make sense of your character or a certain feeling the character has about growing up, then add it to your character before that character enters the stage and after he or she leaves it.

Know what your character is thinking when he is not speaking, *especially* when he is not speaking. This background information doesn't matter to anyone but you, so don't worry about justifying it to anyone else. This is your creative work.

Another important step in the initial phase of character work is dramatic analysis. A dramatic analysis is a technical look into the play. This may include information about the playwright or aspects of production of the play.

Each play may be broken into six divisions which should be studied and analyzed in order for the actor to have full knowledge of the playwright and his intentions, the characters and other elements vital to the play's production. These six divisions are plot, characterization, idea, language and sound, visual elements, and form and spirit.

Plot is chronological structure. Plot is what happens in a play.

Many play reviews fail to assess the play critically but rather give a summary of the plot, which may or may not be an important element of a play. Some plays depend much more on character or visual elements while other plays rely heavily on the plot structure.

Characterization is the element through which the story or plot is revealed. Character may or may not be human and may or may not be realistic. Action and conflict revolve around character. Likewise, dialogue and use of language are products of character.

Idea is the subject of the play. Idea is what the play is about — not in the same sense that plot reveals what a play is about, but rather in a general and unspecific sense. Like theme, idea supports the heart of a play's meaning.

Language and sound create mood, establish character and represent time, place and locale. Each playwright employs a particular type of language and uses specific sounds in the play. Each character also has a particular manner of using language and sound. Language is used to indicate a character's social class or education, to impart a particular tone (lyrical or harsh, for example), or to achieve various other goals. Sounds may include environmental sounds, background sounds or music as part of the play's overall aural image.

Visual elements are those that contribute to the total visual impact of the production. Set decoration, lighting, use of color, props, costume, stage dressing and set design are all part of the total visual picture. Much visual information may be implied by the playwright; if not, the scene designers should be consulted in order to incorporate their visual ideas into the overall creative process.

Form and spirit refers to the style used in writing the play and the sound or essence which permeates the consciousness of the audience. The form of a play may be comedy or tragedy, drama or social comedy, farce or tragicomedy. Form may also include surrealism, absurdism, symbolism, constructivism, or other specific styles. Spirit in simple terms is the impression the audience is left with at the conclusion of the play.

The actor should study and analyze each division as it applies to the play and his own character. Some plays may require outside reading and considerable time invested in order to understand the play and the playwright's intention. In addition, if the actor is working on a play for production the director's concept should be studied carefully so that any additions or deletion in the play's basic structure and message are understood.

Once the actor is sufficiently prepared for further study of the play and his character, work may begin on the steps of the Ten Line Exercise.

The following is an example of the steps of the exercise using the characters from *The Ghost Sonata* by August Strindberg. These are samples of the studies which may help actors to visualize how each step in the Ten Line Exercise can be used. Different actors may wish to use alternative approaches to each of the steps.

The Ghost Sonata by August Strindberg

Cast of Characters

the Old Man
the Student
the Mummy
the Young Lady

THE WORD STUDY

As I studied the main character from this play I observed colors, textures, abstract symbols and emotions among numerous words and word phrases which make up the word list for each character.

The four illustrations of word studies demonstrate the initial reactions I had to the four major characters. It should be noted that an actor could experiment with a variety of methods of compiling the list. Instead of listing the words in columns you may wish to paint the words using various textures, colors and shapes, or you may experiment by grouping the words into specific patterns with no limitations as to the size of the background used. The word list is the point of departure in the process of developing a character utilizing the steps of the Ten Line Exercise and should be referred to often during the entire process of preparing for audition, class work or performance.

THE SOUND STUDY

In preparation for the sound study the actor works with a variety of sounds and the reactions to those sounds. The actor will find

Fig. 10. Word study for the Old Man.

Fig. 11. Word study for the Student.

Fig. 12. Word study for the Mummy.

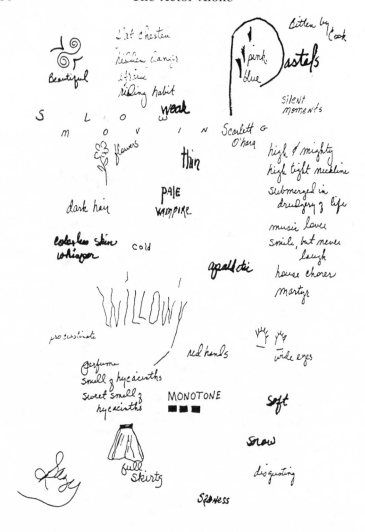

Fig. 13. Word study for the Young Lady.

that this study can be of a personal nature. Now that the actor is working alone he will not have to explain his choice of sounds, so he may explore sounds from his own experiences which relate to those of the character.

The actor working alone may pose questions to the character concerning basic emotional makeup, reactions to other factors or characters in the play and environmental sounds. He then may ask the same questions of himself or inquire how he might feel and react in similar situations. The merging answers can become part of the sound study.

The Old Man

In the process of composing a sound study for this character I first referred to the word list to obtain essential sounds which might have been noted and basic emotional qualities of the character which affect the sounds. The character emerged as a greedy, evil thief who is ultimately judged for his wrongdoings. A strange nightmare aura of darkness, loneliness and evil surrounds the character, and this feeling must be evident in the sound study. I chose to express this strange aura by selecting a sound which indicated an indefinable space. The howling wind refers to the lonely Old Man as he exits somewhere and everywhere. The chipping away of the cement on bricks refers to the destructiveness inherent in the character; the laughter indicates his evil vileness. The sound of the explosion is like the distant thunder heard before a storm, rather than the loud, abrupt explosion at the detonation of dynamite.

Since I chose the theme of judgment as the main idea of the character, the reverberating echo of a gavel is heard. The greed of the character is evidenced by the jingling of coins, symbolic of the character's fate. The repetition of the door slamming evokes a feeling of finality. My sound study looks like this:

soft wind howling (continuously, with intermittent
    periods of intensity)
slowly, and far away, the sounds of someone
methodically chipping away the cement from old
bricks, this sound stops abruptly and the low,
guttural laughter of an old man is heard. The
laughter grows in volume until it is broken by the
sound of. . .

a large explosion in the far distance.
the explosion is repeated and finally the
sound dies away slowly . . .
long silence
the chomping of crackers is heard followed by
repeated periods of silence then chomping . . .
then, distant at first, the sound of a gavel
being pounded on a large desk . . . the sound grows
closer and closer until it is very loud . . .
an abrupt silence . . .
the sound of money jangling, followed by the
sound of greedy laughter, the laughter continues
and is accompanied by the sound of footsteps on a
creaky floor . . .
silence, then parrot sounds . . .
again silence, then the echo of a door being
slammed in slow motion, the repeating of that
sound . . .
the resumption of the solitary wind fades slowly.

I would like to point out that I had certain personal reactions
to many of the sounds presented in this study. The sound of the soft
wind evoked feelings of aloneness and the occasional howling served
to enforce the idea of imminent evil or fear.

Initially the sound of the chipping cement was not annoying,
but as it was repeated it grated on my nerves and I reacted physically. Keeping in mind that the movement study will follow as one
step in the process of the Ten Line Exercise, one should always be
aware of the movement responses to sounds or the movement
responses to visual images.

As you perform or listen to your sound study, allow yourself the
opportunity to become sensitive to any movement related actions or
responses which may occur. I responded to the sound study by flinch-
ing at each recurring sound until the hammering stopped. The
sound of the old man's laugh brought forth many visual images and
vocal sounds.

One surprising reaction I had to the sound exercise was that all
of the sounds took on a slow, dreamlike quality. This slow motion
essence was later interpreted into slow motion movements. This
proved to be the key element in the development of this character.

The Student

I interpreted much of the characterization for the Student through silence. The emotional intensity of the character exists internally and is seldom exhibited externally in a brilliant show of emotion. Silence, therefore, plays a large role in this sound study.

> silence, the sound of pages being turned quietly...
> then the sound of writing as with a script pen...
> these two sounds diminish and are replaced with a soft wind blowing through the trees...
> the sound of someone taking a breath as though for the first smell of spring...
> sudden silence, then the sound of building blocks being placed upon one another and hammering, then the sound of blocks falling...
> again silence, then quiet sobbing...
> as the sobbing fades out the low sound of waltz music is heard, it grows louder and more joyous and is accompanied by the sound of a girl humming...
> the music fades while the humming continues...
> as the sound of a sitar grows in volume, the humming diminishes...the sitar continues as laughter begins then develops into a fearful crying...
> sudden silence, long silence...
> quiet praying and the sound of footsteps retreating...

Again the reactions to the sound study was manifested in physical terms. Each specific sound seemed to indicate a particular movement. One basic difference was noted after completing the Student's sound study. While performing the Old Man's sound exercise I felt placed in an exterior position, on the outside looking in at the character, whereas in the performance of the Student's sound collage I felt introverted and inside looking out. Personal feelings of sympathy for the protagonist could be the reason for this, but these sentiments would be evident to anyone viewing these exercises or portrayal of these characters on the stage.

The Mummy

The sound study for this character required a strange juxtaposition of seemingly unrelated sounds which characterize the Mummy as the most bizarre element of the play. The Mummy also emerges as the most texturally vivid character in terms of sound. The textures of sounds are contrasted with one another. For example, the initial scuffling sound and the stridently mechanical parrot voice, the smooth purr and the creaking chair are all texturally rich. The relatively unrelated sounds of the clock striking and the chomping of biscuits serve to restate the bizarre nature of the Mummy.

the scuffling noise rats make in the process
of building their nests...

then the chomping noise of munching on
crackers...

both these sounds cease and in a parrot voice
the word "What?" is uttered...

silence
repeat "What?"
long pause...

the word "Jacob" is repeated three times, the
first time almost unintelligibly...

after the final "Jacob" the sound of shutting
and locking a large door...it is repeated ten
times, each time growing in volume...

silence
a purring sound which is followed by the
repetition of "Pretty Polly" twice in parrot chatter...

the ominous sound of a clock striking twelve;
each strike it grows louder...

simultaneously with the twelfth strike the
word "Stop!" in a human voice...

long silence
"Jacob" is uttered in a human voice, then in
a mocking parrot voice...

the sound of a creaking rocking chair...
silence

While performing the sound study for this character I found that animal images kept recurring, physically and mentally. Mental pictures of rats gathering bits and pieces and parrots waddling back and forth in their cages accompanied similar physical reactions.

All movements suggested became small, tight and gnarled until the increasingly loud repetition of the word "Jacob." At this point the insignificant size of the parrot began to grow and strengthen.

The movements became rigid and huge, then with the final "Jacob" the mammoth parrot returned to the small crouched figure as the rocking chair was heard creaking. During this sound collage I experienced an overwhelming sense of suspicion and covetousness which ultimately led to an inhuman power and size which lasted momentarily.

The Young Lady

The qualities which are initially observed in this character are freshness, youth and vitality. I chose to relate personal reactions to these same qualities. The use of the sounds of horses galloping and spring wind evoke feelings of vitality and freshness. The mental images produced by these sounds contribute to the character of the Young Lady as she is never seen on stage. The use of personal sound responses invites a greater variety of emotions, activities and situations to arise and permits a character of greater depth to be realized.

This character as written in the text of the play remains one dimensional, but when I explored other attitudes and emotional ranges through the sound study, a multifaceted personality emerged. The sucking sound is symbolic of vampirism, an important image in the play. The banging window shutter and breathlessness restate the drudgery that the character is compelled to live with, and the fresh sounds of spring associated with the horseback riding add dimension to the character. I chose some recorded music, the *Trois Gymnopedies* by Erik Satie, to elicit sympathy and pity.

> the sound of spring wind blowing. . . this is
> accompanied by the sound of a galloping horse. . .
> the sound of the horse fades as laughter is
> heard, this is then accompanied by waltz music. . .
> silence
> the sound of someone walking up stairs, tired
> and breathless. . .

the repetition of only one string of a harp
being plucked. . .it is a sour note. . .
then many strings are plucked and the sound
is more harmonious. . .
laughter tops the harp music and reaches a
furious level. . .
silence
the sound of someone eating an over-ripe
peach. . .
silence
the sound of a shutter banging in the wind of
a vicious storm, it fades slowly. . .
silence
the sound of the striking of a match, someone
blows it out, this is repeated three times. . .
someone strikes the harp, but no sound is
heard. . .
the sound of someone sobbing, breathless
and exhausted. . .
the sound of bells ringing in the distance,
one of the bells suddenly rings sour. . .sobbing
continues. . .
the first movement of Erik Satie's *Trois
Gymnopedies.*

The performance of this sound study elicits a more intellectual
response than the other sound studies. Light colors and lyric sounds
rather than movements or body positions are suggested in response
to the studies. These reactions proved valuable and were interpreted as the character being more physically passive than the other
characters. The Young Lady emerges as a character who does not
move but is moved by others.

Each step of the Ten Line Exercise emerges as a natural out-
growth of the preceding study and flows easily into the next phase.
This may not be true each time the exercise is performed for a
different character. Words suggested in the word study open the
way for the sound study. The sound study suggests movements and
emotional qualities which provide inspiration for the final study.

The studies for *The Ghost Sonata* have remained consistent with
the theme of the play. The surreal dreamlike qualities have been

elaborated on through each character in terms of words, sounds and visual interpretations.

THE VISUAL STUDY

The purpose and procedure of creating a character visual study is to provide a visual sense of the character, including ideas on such elements as silhouette, posture, or environmental decorations which affect the character. These visual studies may take the form of collage, painting, sculpture or nature object.

The visual study could include personal items used to evoke reactions similar to those of the character. The results of using personal items are similar to those of the sound study. While working alone the actor may find more freedom due to the fact that no justification is needed for various personal reactions.

The Old Man

This visual study is best expressed through the medium of collage. The grouping together of a variety of symbols, images and textures exhibits the qualities inherent in the character. For example, the destructiveness of the character is evidenced by the deteriorated building which has been destroyed from within. The shattering of dreams and treacherous texture of the character are exemplified by the broken mirror which plays a significant role in the theme for the play.

The completed collage of the Old Man raises feelings of fear and apprehension in the onlooker. I found that the pieces of broken mirror made me wary of any tactile contact with the collage, and this response was evident as the character interacted with others on stage.

The finished collage kept me mindful of the treacherous, destructive nature of the Old Man (Old Hummel). The greatest effect of the study was in the reactions of other characters toward the Old Man.

The Student

This character symbolizes many positive themes. He is a symbolic Christ figure, a savior and a merciful hero, yet he ultimately destroys the Young Lady out of necessity. I chose to represent this

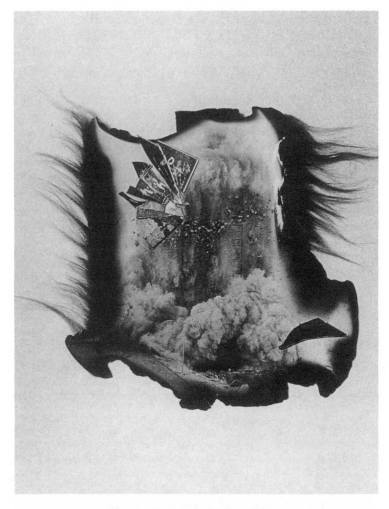

Fig. 14. Visual study for the Old Man.

character through a nature object. The object chosen reflects many qualities inherent in the Student. The jutting outline as pictured in Fig. 15 reflects a dialogue which was developed after physically exploring the line and direction of the character. I walked the line of the silhouette of the object and found that the wavy, rippling lines which add to the texture of the object are representative of the underlying surging emotion of the Student. Through working alone

Fig. 15 and Fig. 16. Two views of a visual study for the Student.

Fig. 17. Visual study for the Mummy.

I was able to respond personally to the tactile exploration of the object.

The Mummy

In composing the visual study for this character a variety of visual elements were considered, and the means of expression of these elements was chosen to be a collage. The visual image most commonly associated with the Mummy is that of a parrot, which is represented by the feathers in the collage.

Another visual element is color and texture. In search of the proper material to express these elements, I looked over the word list and found images of the look, feel and smell of old fabric. I found a piece of faded fabric in an old trunk and the musty smell fit the image of the character. Even though the color was faded it expressed a sense of lost power.

The feathers represented the bird-like frailty and added a soft, delicate quality to the caged figure. The dark, almost despondent quality of the color reminded me of the power possessed by the Mummy though these qualities were not seen in the character's physical makeup.

Fig. 18. Visual study for the Young Lady: *Phenomena Astral Signal* **by Paul Jenkins.**

The Young Lady

The painting entitled *Phenomena Astral Signal* by Paul Jenkins was chosen to represent the visual qualities of the Young Lady. The colors, the flat texture and the deep sordid center of the painting all suggest details inherent in this character. The colors at the outer edges of the painting reflect her young, willowy, fresh quality; the dark, stormy colors at the center of the work hint at her unseen vampirism.

One is free to arrive at any interpretation upon observing the Jenkins painting. Some may see a bird in flight; others may perceive flames. Whatever the explanation, certain qualities emerge predominant.

I found that in developing visual compositions for the characters of the Old Man and the Mummy ideas and images first presented themselves, and the study required a compiling of differing textures, colors and images. Specific visual pieces and characteristics associated with the characters came to mind while working on the Young Lady and the Student. It may be said that for the Old Man and the Mummy specifics came first and then the collage, and in the case of the Student and the Young Lady, the object and painting came first and specifics later.

What relation this plays in the development of any of these characteristics for the stage may be explained by the fact that some characters lend themselves more readily to visual studies. The collage, nature object or painting may result in discovery of unknown elements, but in the case of the Student and the Young Lady it provided a visual composition which possessed the same qualities such as color, texture, and emotional associations.

The Movement Study

The movement study, which explores the emotional as well as the physical characteristics of the character, provides an important link to the final phase of the Ten Line Exercise. The movement study furnishes the blueprint for the final exercise, providing a transition from one line or level of emotion to another.

In the movement study the actor may explore movement patterns, movement habits and clichés, and movement qualities of the character through either realistic or abstract means. The actor may begin his movement study by classifying the character according to the movements which are apparent in the mental and physical personality of the role. The actor should then explore the internal and external tensions resulting from the study. One way to conduct the movement study is to classify the movements according to the effort

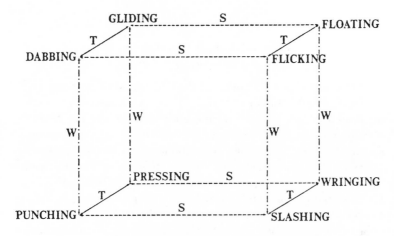

Fig. 19. Rudolf Laban's effort diagram.

theory of Rudolf Laban. This need not imply a thorough study of Laban's many theories; a familiarity with the effort vocabulary will suffice.

Laban classified all human movement into categories called efforts. In movement energy is expended. This exerted energy emphasizes four motion factors: flow, weight, time and space. The inner or psychological motivation which precedes movement is significant to the dramatic actor, and the effort classification of movement provides the actor with a viable description of psychological and physical movements.

The efforts may be outlined according to the motion factors defining each effort. The efforts are punch, slash, dab, flick, press, wring, glide and float. Punch is straight in direction of flow, heavy in weight, and fast in time. Slash is curved, heavy and fast; dab is straight, light and fast; while flick is curved, light and fast. Press, wring, glide and float are all slow in time, yet they differ in space and weight. Press is straight and heavy; wring is curved and heavy; glide is straight and light; and float is curved and light.

Movements as well as attitudes, vocal patterns and work actions can be classified according to a specific effort. The efforts provide the actor with a working vocabulary through which he can clearly communicate the essence of an intended attitude or movement.

The Laban effort vocabulary is useful because it provides apt descriptions for movements and attitudes both mental and physical.

The Old Man

Predominant physical effort: wring
Predominant mental effort: punch/press

The hunchback silhouette of the Old Man is seen as the study opens. The Old Man does not move for a long time except to cock his head from side to side intermittently as though he has heard or seen something. His arms hang freely and his figure is suspiciously sinister as it remains relatively stationary. He limps grotesquely toward a chair and seats himself and soon spies something approaching him. It is a figure that frightens him. He tries to rise from his chair but cannot. The figure draws closer and closer as the attitudes of wring dominate his movements. He continues to wring until he falls from his chair and tries to scramble away. Finally he buries his head, and, seeing that the figure is gone, he rises. Now he stands straight and tall and walks unafraid. The Old Man takes a few steps; then, as though hearing something or someone behind him, he turns slowly. It is the same figure again. He retreats slowly, shaking his head "No." He begins to press against the invisible force—first with his arms, then with his shoulders, then with his whole body. He is soon overcome and falls to the floor as though being beaten.

The Student

Predominant physical effort: glide/flick
Predominant mental effort: wring

The study opens with the Student walking briskly as though on a sunny spring day. He stops periodically to remove his jacket and to tie a shoe. As he continues to walk he encounters a peculiar scene. It is as though some large structure is falling or caving in, and he tries to prevent this disaster by supporting the imaginary ceiling. The physical attitude of press is used until finally his strength diminishes and he struggles under the weight of the structure. Then, as though the burden is placed on his shoulders, he begins to move away, giving the effect of Christ carrying the cross. The Student continues with his burden until ahead he sees a vision. He slowly straightens and the imaginary weight of the cross vanishes. He approaches the vision and extends his hand. He kneels and mimes picking flowers and gathering them into a bouquet. The offering of flowers to the vision is rebuked and he begins to assume the attitude of wring. The study in wring slowly subsides and he rises, walks away and extends his arms with his head high as though toward a religious idol.

The Mummy

> *Predominant physical effort: dab/flick*
> *Predominant mental effort: slash*

The study opens with the character impersonating a parrot with her arms folded up (hands under armpits and elbows extended outward) and clawed feet characteristically scratching away at imaginary soil. Initially the mime of the parrot is as realistic as possible and possesses certain unavoidable comic overtones. Particular attention is given to the elbows, feet and head, which is strained forward. The bird is scratching away at the soil looking for food. Suddenly a morsel is spotted and the character drops to her knees and continues to search, but now with her elbows. Then, forgetting the search for food, the Mummy looks up and realizes a cage surrounds her. A slow transformation occurs as she rises and sheds the birdlike movements and assumes a human stance. Through mime the Mummy approaches many of the bars and touches them, testing their strength but not as yet trying to escape. Then her arms fold slowly again into a winglike position and, gradually becoming angry, she tries to separate the bars using her wings as hands. The intensity of the movements increases and she takes on the attitudes of slash. As the slashing movements continue her arms unfold, leaving the caged human slashing in anger and frustration. Abruptly all movements cease and the Mummy makes one large, slow, sweeping movement with the right arm/wing and the imaginary cage is gone. The Mummy is not surprised at this and turns and walks slowly in the opposite direction. She slowly assumes the birdlike silhouette exactly as it was in the opening of the study.

The Young Lady

> *Predominant physical effort: float/slash*
> *Predominant mental effort: wring*

The study begins with the character standing in a motionless position (zero position). Slowly she begins to waltz with free movements and no particular pattern of movement. Suddenly and abruptly the waltzing ceases and the Young Lady crumples to the floor, assuming the attitudes of wring. As the Young Lady strives to overcome the emotional attitude of wring she starts a realistic sweeping movement. Initially it is a mime of sweeping, but gradually she becomes increasingly tired and breathless and the sweeping becomes more abstract. The abstract sweeping movements become larger, faster and heavier until the attitude of slash predominates. The study of slash continues until the Young Lady is completely exhausted and slumps to the floor.

The movement study is of great importance because it is the first point at which the actor can actually bring physical life to the role. Until this point the actor has been dealing in intellectual images, written words and sounds. Admittedly the movement study may be difficult for those who are not accustomed to expression through their bodies, but it is at this stage that the actual character takes on moving, living shape.

Ultimately the actor *must* move, and this step allows him the opportunity to select pieces from preceding studies and place them on the skeleton of his own body, transforming them into a specific character. I found that I gained most from this part of the study. This could be because of my background in dance and stage movement, but any actor can learn to explore the character from a movement perspective.

The movement study not only reinforces the sound, word and visual images but also opens up new horizons of structural, intellectual and technical discoveries.

Upon initially performing the movement studies for each character I experienced emotions which were manifested in external movement tensions. Emotions, instincts and subliminal drives were realized. After numerous repetitions of each character's study the movements seemed to indicate words and dialogue. This response proved true in each of the four characters. For example, there are no specific attitudes in the study of the Old Man which may require him to say "no" or "Who's there?" Dialogue can easily be imagined as the Student picks the flowers and is rebuked, and one can hear the Young Lady speak of the drudgery of life. This tendency to add dialogue should, however, be gently discouraged at this time. This is intended to be not an improvisation exercise, but rather an investigation of movements which will later be coupled with specific lines from the play.

All of the information gained thus far can be integrated into the physical reality of the character. If the actor is actually preparing any of these roles for the stage, this point in the Ten Line Exercise can be equated with the time the actor is off book (has his lines memorized) and setting his role. But before continuing the culmination of all responses into a single study the actor may investigate any additional areas in which he needs more information.

THE CHOICE STUDY

The choice study offers the actor the freedom to explore any area for which he feels additional study is needed. Any previous study may be repeated in greater depth and any research on a particular topic may be conducted to add to the actor's knowledge of the character.

The choice study provides the actor an opportunity to explore movement on a more advanced level should the character dance or have unusual movement habits in the play. Historical research could prove helpful if the character actually lived in a particular time in history. The actor may find it helpful to study any specific dialects, accents or foreign languages that are a necessary part of the role.

The Old Man

The Old Man is most strongly presented as "everyman." Like evil or death, he lurks anywhere and everywhere and is not confined to time or space. It is for this reason that I chose specific lines from the poem "Passenger Pigeons" by Robinson Jeffers to illustrate the choice exercise. The poem spans centuries and in a speculative way extends into the future. It is likely that the Old Man will be reincarnated (as expressed in Buddhist philosophy, an important theme in the play) and live to destroy again. I chose this poem as an imaginary dialogue between the Student and the Old Man. The ultimate end of humanity at man's own hand is evident in the final knowing smile of the death figure in the poem. It was Strindberg's belief that the only escape from the ugliness of life was death, and likewise the poem suggests the only escape from our miserable mistakes is death. Space does not permit reproduction of the entire poem here, but the following excerpt is representative of the ways in which the poem sheds light on the character of the Old Man.

They became too many, they are all dead, / not one remains. / . . . But turn your great rolling eyes away from
humanity, / Those grossly crawling black eyes. It is true we
increase. / . . . Bones that have twitched and quivered and
hung slack in sorrow, coward bones / Worn out with
trembling, strong bones broken on the rock, / . . . Roll
those idiot black eyes of yours / On the field-beasts, not on
intelligent man, / " . . . You'll live forever" — grinning like a
skull, covering his mouth with / his hand — "What could ex-
terminate you?"[45]

The Student

Many times in the third scene of *The Ghost Sonata* the Student
makes a direct reference to Buddhism and Buddhist philosophy.
Strindberg himself was a student of Buddhism and its influence is
evident in the Student's mentioning the cosmos and in the final
prayer. In further research of the character of the Student I chose
to investigate Buddhist principles theology. The Four Noble Truths
and the idea that suffering is inherent in all bodily existence were
especially helpful in understanding the character. The principles of
the Eightfold Path and reincarnation are evident in the theme of the
play and the character of the Student. The Student possesses second
sight and could be considered an "enlightened one."

The Mummy

The study chosen for the Mummy focuses on vampirism, the
subject of the play. In this play one either is a vampire or is affected
by vampires, and the myths and stories in folklore concerning vampirism give beneficial information to the actor in his preparation of
this role.

The Mummy and the Student are two characters that possess
the power and courage to destroy the vampires. The stake driven
through the heart of the Old Man is symbolic of his confrontation
with the truth. If the Student is considered a Christ figure it is likely
that the Old Man is a devil figure. The images of devil and vampire
are closely associated with the word "demon."

The image of a demon is an important aspect of the character,
and research revealed some interesting and helpful insight. Origin-
ally the word "demon" had positive as well as negative connotations.

Primitive peoples believed that even the most benevolent spirits had malicious moments. Rites were often performed to intercede with the spirits to overcome their "bad" times. The early Christians were the first to associate demons with the devil. The ancient Teutons believed that the soul of the dead returned by night, often in form of wind, rain or storms. Demons often tormented the living during their sleep, hence the terms "night-rider" and "night-mare." These same demonic spirits also rode on animals, sat on people's breasts to suffocate them, and sucked the milk from women and cows. Demons were described as crouching, as having an "evil eye," and as being bearers of bad luck.

This research on vampires and demons provides insight into the characters and the play as a whole. The images lend helpful ideas which influence movements and sounds of the characters.

The Young Lady

There is little dialogue and physical action written in the script for the Young Lady. The actor is free to create a character from his imagination as only slight guidelines are provided by Strindberg. Due to the lack of specific character traits, the actor faces the problem of giving the character dimension. For this reason I chose to repeat the movement study with particular emphasis directed toward the images reported in the third scene. The Young Lady speaks of "the drudgery of life" and this movement study focuses on the abstraction of household chores. The medium used to express these abstracted movements was first inspired by the New York production of *The Life and Times of Joseph Stalin* by Robert Wilson and later in the Dallas Theatre Center's production of *Jack Ruby: All American Boy* directed by Paul Baker. In these productions slow motion was used to increase tension, provide visual starkness, and highlight and heighten the effects of movement onstage. For example, simple movements such as bending down to retrieve an object would require fifteen minutes instead of the usual few seconds. In particular, in the scene from *Jack Ruby* in which Lee Harvey Oswald is killed, the action takes place over an extended period of time, thus increasing the tension and anxiety of an event the audience knows will occur. By using this technique the singular movement of the actor is dramatically intensified and movement series are dissected so that they may be analyzed.

The movement study as part of the choice study for the character of the Young Lady consisted of a series of common household duties: dusting, sweeping, scrubbing floors and ironing. Each task was conducted as realistically as possible in slow motion. This feat required a great deal of balance and endurance. For example, in the process of ironing, each forward stroke of the iron was drawn out into many minutes. The result was a new and more vivid meaning of the drudgery spoken of by the Young Lady.

By working alone I had the space of my own home for experimentation, so I was not restricted by time or environment. The study involved feelings of exhaustion, frustration and boredom, all experienced by the Young Lady.

THE TEN LINE STUDY

The ten line study is the final component of the Ten Line Exercise. It is, in effect, the entire play as demonstrated by the progressions made by a single character throughout his life as the character. Each line is chosen to illustrate an emotion, a situation, a relationship or a progression made by the character. The transitions may be composed of sound or movement.

In preparation for the ten line study it was found to be most beneficial to first return to the movement study, which usually reflects a variety of facets of the character and any physical responses to various events or personalities in the play.

It was stated earlier that the movement study provides a blueprint for this final study, but this remark does not imply that the movement exercise is superimposed onto the ten chosen lines. On the contrary, one initiates the ten line study by selecting the ten appropriate lines which indicate the spectrum of a character's experience.

Ten lines is a somewhat arbitrary number; some characters might require more and others fewer. Nine lines could work, or twelve or fifteen. The point is to select a minimum number of lines which focus on turning points or high points in the life of the character on stage. In the case of long speeches or stories by the character, the actor might look for one key line of that monologue, or perhaps a line preceding or following the monologue might offer a key to the pervading emotion of that moment for the character.

The ten line study provides an unusual opportunity for actors to develop a rich character for so-called small parts or parts in which the character has few or no lines. The number of lines or words spoken in this study should not be of prime consideration.

Once the specific lines are chosen the actor may review the movement study and note any internal or external attitudes which reflect or contrast to any one of the chosen lines. In the initial stage of preparation in the study, the actor may experiment by repeating the sound study as he examines the lines, or the actor may perform the movement study while reciting the lines. The study will be refined and the unnecessary or irrelevant sounds and movements may be discarded. "The final ten line study will portray a great many more facets because of the incorporation of other dramatic elements, both visual and auditory."[46]

The Old Man

The hunchback silhouette is stationary. As he begins to move he slowly heads for the chair. His predominant effort is wring. He is jingling change in his pockets and laughing quietly. He begins to mime speaking to someone.

"When I was a young man I had a friend who wouldn't pronounce window, he always said 'winder.'"

He slowly extends his gnarled hand and slowly shakes the hand of the imaginary person to whom he is speaking.

"My name is Hummel."

He rises from his chair as though tired and takes a few short steps as he indicates a house to his left.

"I too am very fond of that house . . . but not in the way you think. . . ."

Suddenly he stoops down and begins to chisel away the mortar from an imaginary brick. He looks about him suspiciously, then begins to laugh loudly.

"But no one knows me, not really. . . . I take a great interest in human destinies. . . ."

He rises and looks approvingly at his work and returns to his chair.

"Very well, I may not have second sight, but I have other powers."

Suddenly, to his right, he sees a vision and he shrinks to his chair. As the vision approaches his fear increases and he extends his hands

toward the vision as if asking for mercy. Then he turns to his compan-
ion and begs.

"Don't leave me, I beg you—I'm tired, I'm lonely—but it hasn't always been this way, I tell you. I have an infinitely long life behind me—infinitely long—I've made people unhappy—people have made me unhappy, the one cancels out the other."

He falls from his chair and curls up in fright.

"But before I die I want to make you happy. . . . Our destinies are tangled. . . ."

Suddenly he realizes that the vision is gone and he is helped to his chair by his companion.

"But I can open doors—and hearts—if only I can find an arm to do my will. Serve me, and you shall be a lord of creation."

He begins to smile and laughs, and he looks around confidently. He rises and stands taller than before. He takes a few steps and listens intently. He whispers.

"I prefer silence . . . in which one can hear thoughts and see the past. Silence cannot hide anything—which is more than you can say of words."

He points, using slashing movements, to an imaginary group of people in front of him. He yells at them accusingly.

"The mask is ripped from the imposter and the villain stands exposed . . . extraordinary, how silent you all are!"

Quickly he hears something behind him and in one jerky move turns and is overcome with fear. He struggles to be brave.

"Clocks can strike!—and I can strike too. . . . Clocks can strike! Coo-coo! Coo-coo!"

His body slowly crumbles until he is a mass on the floor.

The Student

He walks briskly and takes off his jacket, tie and shoes. He notices his reflection in a store window.

"So that's me! What do you know?"

He continues walking until he sees a house.

"I went by there yesterday, when the sun was glittering on the panes—I dreamed of all the beauty and luxury there must be in that house, I said to my friend, "Imagine having an apartment there, four flights up, and a beautiful wife, and two pretty kids, and 20 thousand crowns in dividends every year.""

Someone approaches him and he congenially shakes hands only to be frightened by the iciness of the handshake.

"Sunday child, did you say? I was actually born on a Sunday, so I am told."

He moves away as though in a dream and begins to mime the story as he tells it.

". . . Then I noticed a crack in the wall. I could hear the floor beams snapping in two. . . . The next moment the house collapsed. . . . I escaped—but in my arms—where I thought I had a child—there wasn't anything. . . ."

By the end of the story he is in anguish, which is evident by the predominant wring movements, and he looks up to see an imaginary Young Lady. He picks illusionary flowers and presents them to her.

"I love it above all other flowers—its stem rising straight and slender, like a young maiden's, from the round bulb, which floats on water and reaches its white rare roots down into clear, colorless nothingness."

The Young Lady has not accepted the bouquet and he again presents them to her. Still she resists and in frustration he slowly says,

"Sometimes there comes over me a crazy desire to say everything I'm thinking."

In anger and retaliation he rises and knowingly condemns her in the story.

"It was a Sunday morning, and I stood looking into these rooms. I saw a Colonel who wasn't a Colonel. I had a magnanimous benefactor who turned out to be a bandit and had to hang himself. I saw a mummy who wasn't one, and a maiden who—."

Realizing what he has done to the Young Lady (she is dead) he picks up the flowers.

"Where is beauty to be found; . . . where do honor and faith exist; where can you find anything that fulfills its faults, and by a love without flaw. . . ."

He slowly retreats and begins to recite the verse while extending his arms outstretched to the side so that the image of Christ on the cross is illustrated.

"I saw the sun/ And from its blaze/ There burst on me/ The deepest truth; . . ."

The Mummy

She has assumed the tight, constricted movements of a parrot. Abruptly she turns and as though surprised, she angrily snaps in a parrot voice,

"Why do you open the door? Didn't I tell you to keep it closed?"

She begins to scratch in the soil as though looking for food.

"Pretty Polly! You there, Jacob?"

She makes chattering noises but stops as she sees someone enter. She gradually straightens and assumes the stature of a human.

"Yes, this is how I look! — And that's how I did look once upon a time. Life gives one a great education."

She is angry and tense and reaches for the person to whom she has been talking. Suddenly and feverishly she realizes that she is confined. She begins to try to separate the bars using her hands until gradually she again assumes the parrotlike stance and begins to pry the bars apart, using her arms as wings.

"Keep your hands off her, I warn you, or you'll die."

She has been using her parrot voice but suddenly she becomes human again and with one large sweeping gesture dissolves the bars.

"Our crimes and our secrets and our guilt binds us together! We have split up and gone our separate ways an infinite number of times. But we're always drawn back together again. . . ."

She has been encircling her victim and now begins to engulf him with her arms until she has captured him in her hands. Now his size is diminishing until he vanishes.

"But I can stop time in its course. I can wipe out the past, and undo what is done. Not with bribes, not with threats — but through suffering and repentance."

She wrings her hands and opens her palms and examines their emptiness. She returns to her cage and closes the door.

"We are poor miserable creatures, we know that."

She again assumes the birdlike posture and scratches in the dirt, repeating in her parrot voice,

"Pretty bird! Where's Jacob?"

The Young Lady

The initial movements are free and open as the Young Lady waltzes and laughs. She breathlessly ceases her dancing and sits on the floor and speaks to someone on her left.

"Now you must sing a song to my flowers."
She begins to hum a lullaby and the sadness of the song increases. She becomes worried and suddenly rises to go.
"Time-testing patience."
She begins to explain her actions to her companion.
"To be awakened in the middle of the night, to have . . . [*she goes to an imaginary window*] to get up and close the banging window—which the housemaid forgot to close. . . . To climb up on a ladder to fix the damper on the stovepipe after the maid broke off the cord."
She falls onto her knees and begins to mime scrubbing floors. Her emotions are futile and apatheic. Her weakness increases and as someone tries to make her rise, she refuses.
"First comes the drudgery of life, the drudgery of keeping oneself above the dirt of life."
Finally, exhausted, she rises.
"Living is such a nuisance, and I get so tired at times."
Suddenly, as though seeing someone who frightens her, she shakes her head, "No." She shrinks away and assumes wring characteristics. She falls to the floor.
"Bring the screen quickly! I'm dying."

The fact that each phase of the Ten Line Exercise has now been executed does not mean that the character is now ready for the stage. The actor has been building a strong foundation and with each additional study has increased his knowledge, assuming mannerisms, vocal inflections, body tensions and personality insight. The word study, sound study and visual study served as foundations to which the framework provided by the movement study was added.

At this point many of the responses from the initial studies may be unconscious. The actor should have a wide range of minute characteristics in his mind and should utilize them, consciously and unconsciously, in the final ten line study. For example, in the word study of the Old Man his hunchback posture, gnarled appearance, hoarseness and eavesdropping were noted, and each is an integral part of the ten line study.

The tensions noted in the movement study have been duplicated, but now have also affected the delivery of the lines. The ugly, hoarse, hissing sounds so evident in the word list and sound study are evident in the first lines of the ten line study. The "s" in "was," "always" and "said" is altered because of the insight gained in those early studies. Also, the other characters in the play have specific reactions to Hummel because of the treachery displayed in the visual study. The character of the Old Man has emerged as a vocally textured giant. His movements are slow and heavy, yet one must always feel as though he is striking out—not in a physical way, but in a cunning, destructive, evil manner.

The Student appears to be a likable person, one who is seen every day, yet there must be a sense of universal sadness about him. Early in the Ten Line Exercise the most conclusive element in the Student was found to be silence. The likable fellow is evident in the opening of the ten line study, but with the third line of the study the character emerges. His rhythm is smooth, his effort attitude is glide and he is in no way aggressive. The smooth evenness of his rhythm, which was first evident in the movement study, now has presented itself in the line delivery. By his fourth line his suffering and pain are beginning to be visible, and unlike the Old Man, he does not hide these agonizing revelations.

The movements of the Mummy most directly affect her line delivery. She fluctuates from human stance and human voice to jerky, birdlike tensions which are vocalized in a tight, constricted, parrotlike voice. The images of parrots with their characteristic chatter, scratching and stance remain vivid in the actor's mind during the performance of the ten line study. Otherwise the character of the Mummy might emerge as an old woman with little of the bizarreness and eeriness that Strindberg intended. It is true for any character that when any tension is applied to the body it will also show its effect on the voice and the delivery of a specific line. It is especially true for the character of the Mummy. She is a paradox of rhythms and textures, both vocal and physical.

The Young Lady, like the Student, first appears similar to many young girls, fresh, vital and gay. Yet, in the movements preceding the first line delivery, she seems a slow moving, oppressed victim. The images noted in the word list such as willowy and monotone certainly manifest themselves in her movements and voice. The painting used in the visual study for the Young Lady adds to the internal and intellectual quality for the character. The breathless, exhausting results of the choice exercise most support the actor in the ten line study. In the final lines of the study it is almost impossible to move, gesture or speak. The physical tensions imposed on the body directly affect the character's breathing and consequently her line delivery.

With the ten line study the actor is now ready "with a vocabulary of hundreds, perhaps thousands, of ideas, word perceptions, and feelings about the character and his own abilities of difficulties in portraying them"[47] to gain further information for rehearsal with the addition of director, designer and other actors.

The creation of a character should not be a finite process. People change in everyday living. They are shaped by experiences, relationships and time. Likewise, the actor creating a role will be flexible. Specific guidelines are provided in the form of stage space and the nonflexible text of the script. These are technicalities which must be reckoned with for the sake of any production as a whole.

In the execution of the steps of the Ten Line Exercise, the actor is taught above all that the creation of a character is an ongoing process. One does not simply learn what to say and where to move once it is said. In other words,

> movement does not stop when vocal delivery is begun and vice-versa. The delivery of the line is part of the character you have spent so much time developing, not an isolated or special technical thing to be tacked on. This is the central point of all the earlier exercises — the unification of voice, body, intelligence and imagination. . . .[48]

Acting is more than recitation of words. Robert Edmond Jones states in the *The Dramatic Imagination*,

> Acting is a process of incarnation. Just that. And it is a miracle. I have no words to express what I feel about this subtle, ancient, sacred art — the marvel of it, the wonder, the meaning. . . . The actor creates in his living self. And just as the good designer retires in favor of the actor, so does the actor withdraw his personal self in favor of the character he is playing. He steps aside. The character lives in him.[49]

The Ten Line Exercise helps the actor to gain a sense of entirety for his character. This sense of entirety cannot be achieved in a short period of time, and its importance is explained by Michael Chekhov in *To the Actor*.

> If in the beginning or from the very first entrance you already have a vision of yourself playing (or rehearsing) your last scene — and, conversely, remembering the first scene as you play (or rehearse) the very last scenes — you will better be able to see your whole part in every detail, as though you were viewing it in perspective from some elevation. The ability to evaluate the details within the part as a well-integrated whole will further enable you to play each of these details as little entities which blend harmoniously into the all embracing entirety.[50]

Each human being is unique and possesses creative gifts. These gifts may be presented to the world to make it more beautiful or progressive, or, in the case of the theatre artist, to define the meanings of human existence in a variety of styles. The actor must seek his own creative path and develop proficiency of body, voice and mind.

This book explores one such creative path. The ultimate beginning and end of this exercise lie in the individual's knowledge of himself and his dedication to the exploration of a dramatic character.

Through the freedom provided by this exercise the actor investigates and examines the skeleton created by the playwright. The actor then summons his knowledge gained in movement and subconscious impressions to breathe life into that skeleton and produce a living personality suspended in time and caught in the space of the theatre.

For an actor, more than for an artist in other fields, work at home is indispensable.

Whereas a singer has to be concerned only with his voice and breathing, a dancer with his physical apparatus, and a pianist with his hands or a wind instrumentalist with his breathing and lip technique—an actor is responsible . . . for his arms, his legs, his eyes, his face, the plasticity of his whole body, his rhythm, his motion. . . . The great majority of actors are convinced that they need to work only at rehearsals and that at home they can enjoy their leisure. But this is not so. In rehearsals the actor merely clarifies the work he should be doing at home.

—CONSTANTIN STANISLAVSKI

V

WORK IN PROGRESS

Whether you are preparing a role for a class assignment, audition, rehearsal or performance the studies in the Ten Line Exercise can give you a valuable link to the inner life and outer manifestations of your character.

Remember, each phase of the Ten Line Exercise can be done alone, without the assistance of coach, fellow actor or director. There are times when you may not have access to others for critique.

The Ten Line Exercise can also be performed as a part of classroom exercises under the supervision of a teacher or coach. In this case you can learn how the character is communicated from the feedback of the class. If suggestions are made, follow them. If certain aspects of the character are unclear, ask for suggestions or comments. Classmates can be a valuable tool in the development of a character. Be certain that everyone in the class understands that you are presenting work in progress and not a finished product ready for performance.

The studies in the Ten Line Exercise can be especially beneficial in a rehearsal setting if the director encourages each member of the cast to use these studies as part of the rehearsal process. Few directors have the time to organize this type of creative exercise as part of a tight rehearsal schedule. Even fewer directors are willing to provide indepth guidance in preparation of a role. Television and stage actor Randy Moore of the Dallas Theatre Center resident company once stated, "Perhaps one out of ten directors will give you any help." He was not exaggerating.

The Ten Line Exercise gives you a direction, a kind of road map to follow in the development of your character. If you get lost it points out a way to get back on the right road. You have to depend on yourself, and the products of the exercise come from your own reactions and inner feelings about the character—his motivation, his relationships and, most important, his life within the context of the play.

The following are workbook suggestions for each study in the Ten Line Exercise. Each study provides questions to ask of your character, points to consider about your own relationship to the character, and other stimuli which may provide valuable insight into the role. Feel free to add to the list if necessary.

The Word Study

Character _____

Play _____

Playwright _____

(You may list, draw, paint or scribble words, word phrases, or word associations with the character. You are encouraged to experiment with the manner in which you record the words. Be aware of abstract images that may come up as you expand your list.)

What are my character's:

likes _____

dislikes _____

favorite colors _____

favorite foods _____

What are my character's physical traits? _____

Tall? Short? Thin? Obese? Walk with a limp? Walk with short steps? Free flowing gestures? Limited or uptight mannerisms?

What does my character look like? _____
Attractive? Athletic? Proud? Younger than his/her years? Muscular? Willowy?

What are some of my character's idiosyncrasies or mannerisms? *Biting nails? Crooked smile? Plays with hair? Left-handed or right-handed? Smokes cigarettes or cigars? Squints? Hands on hips or arms crossed across chest?*

What are some of my character's psychological traits?

_____

Worrisome? Self-centered? Low self-esteem? Victim? Martyr? Belief in God or supreme being? Depressed?

What are some biographical and experiential traits of my character? *Only child? Siblings? Hometown? Home country? Time of history? Happy childhood? Trauma or tragedy in youth, or adolescence? Married? Educational background? Occupation or career?*

How does your character feel about the following:

money _____

power_____

sex _____

death _____

food or drink_____

his/her parents _____

his/her spouse or children _____

significant inanimate objects _____

time _____

home _____

What is my character afraid of? _____
What does my character want? _____
From other? From himself/herself? From life? At any moment in the play?

Describe the rhythm of your character's

walk _____

hand and arm movements _____

speech _____

thinking_____

overall pattern of movement _____

Relate your character in movement, rhythm or appearance to an animal or inanimate object. _____

Birdlike? Catlike? Innocent like a rose? Snowy hair? Staccato speech?

The Sound Study

Character _____

Play _____

Playwright _____

(Look first at the word study for any listing of sounds. Remember that sounds may be environmental, musical, auditory or rhythmic. Avoid spoken words or long passages of dialogue. The purpose of the sound study is to provide a backdrop or "soundtrack" of your character within the context of the play.)

What are the sounds in the environment of the character?

_____

Are there machine sounds? Kitchen sounds? Sounds of babies crying or children playing? Office sounds? Heavy doors slamming? Creaky doors or furniture?

What sounds does the character bring to the environment?

_____

Does the character walk with a heavy walk? High-heeled shoes? Soft-soled shoes? Does the character walk on wooden floors? Concrete?

What sounds does the character make? _____
Bawdy laughter? Giggle? Does the character hum or sing? Does the

*character whistle or make other vocal sounds? Does the character
make audible sounds as they move, stretch, or cry?*

Are musical sounds a part of the play?_____
*Is music played on a musical instrument? A radio or television? Is
music or singing a part of the play?*

What are the sounds that express the psychological or emotional
state of the character at various times in the play?
_____

*Crying? Screaming? Laughing? Grunting? Gasping or breathing in
surprise? Disgust? Grief? Delight?*

What are sounds that other characters express, mechanically or
psychologically, in the play?
_____

In your sound study, do psychological, mechanical, environmental
or musical sounds dominate?

Does your sound study present an overall character profile?

Does your sound study present a backdrop, in chronological order,
for the play?

The sound study may be recorded or performed live, or a combination of both. Remember, the sound study should present a character
profile. What is communicated through the study? What aspects of
the character or the character's life within the context of the play are
expressed in sound?

The Visual Study

Character _____

Play _____

Playwright _____

(Review the word study for visual descriptions of the character. Feel
free to interpret the character in any visual means you feel like exploring: paint, collage, sculpture, object of nature, or inanimate
object.)

What are the colors and textures that express the character?

_____

Muted colors? Vibrant colors? True value colors? Soft, pastel colors?
Smooth texture? Gritty? Rough?

What is the silhouette of the character? _____
How does line express the character? _____

Jagged lines? Curved lines? Aimless, circular lines? Straight lines?

Is the character best expressed in a three dimensional form?
What media best express the character in three dimensionality?
Is the character best expressed in abstract visual style?
What colors? patterns? shapes? concrete images?
Can your character be expressed in an object of nature?
What are the visual rhythms of the object? Are they similar to those
of the character?
What similar visual qualities does your character share with a sea
shell? a piece of bone? a leaf? a stone?
What does the visual study communicate about your character?

The Movement Study

Character _____

Play _____

Playwright _____

(Review the word study for suggestions of movement patterns,
movement habits, movement styles, gestures and mannerisms. Remember to consider abstract movements which may express
psychological or emotional traits.)

What are some specific actions that the character performs in the
play?

_____

Work actions? Household chores? Personal grooming habits?

How does the character handle objects in the play? _____

Keys? Eating utensils and food or drink? Cigarettes, cigars or pipes?
Eyeglasses and other personal items?

Can you walk through the actions of your character scene by scene
for the entire play?
Can you walk through the actions of your character in slow motion?
What abstract movements express psychological or emotional traits
of the character?
Is the psychological or inner character flick? Glide? Press?
Are the abstract movements slow? Fast? Heavy? Light? Straight?
Curved?
Prepare a movement study which expresses the physical as well as
psychological life of the character. Use abstract movements or move-
ment patterns as transitions from one movement to the next.

The Choice Study

Character _____

Play _____

Playwright _____

(Review the play for aspects that may need further study. Remember
that you may repeat any of the previous studies for more in-depth
work.)

Are you familiar with the time period in which the play is set? If not,
consider reading novels, poetry or nonfiction to give you a better
understanding of the time period, the social mores, and the beliefs
of the time period.
What fiction works are set in the same period? _____
What works of visual art are from the period? _____
What music is from the period? _____
Are there films set during the same period? _____
Are you familiar with all of the language used in the play?
Make a list of words or word phrases with which you are unfamiliar.
Are there words or word phrases of which you have a semantic
misunderstanding?
Are there special activities or abilities that you must have to portray
the part?

Play a musical instrument? Dance? Handcrafts? Is the character physically handicapped?
If you repeat one of the previous studies what are you trying to achieve?

The Ten Line Study

Character _____

Play _____

Playwright _____

(The ten line study is a performance of the character in the complete play but in condensed form. Various lines from the play provide "moments," turning points, conflicts, crises or degrees of change in the life of the character. These moments from the play may be accompanied with images or elements from the sound, visual or movement studies. You are encouraged to use abstract movements or sounds to illustrate psychological traits in the character. Actual sounds and movements will give the study a feeling of performance and realism.)
Choose approximately ten lines from various scenes of the play that place your character in a different emotional, psychological or physical state. (If your character does not have a large number of lines from which to choose, do choose ten moments of inner change in the character. These inner changes may or may not occur within the character as he/she is on stage.)

Line 1_____

Line 2 _____

Line 3 _____

Line 4 _____

Line 5 _____

Line 6 _____

Line 7 _____

Line 8 _____

Line 9 _____

Line 10 _____

What are the physical actions that occur during the line in the play?
What is the psychological or emotional state of the character during
the line?
What sounds or movements can provide time for a progression of the
character from one state or plane of feeling to another?
Do you feel that you express the complete character in the performance of the ten line study?

The following are examples of students' work in progress in all
stages of the Ten Line Exercise. These students come from a variety
of theatre backgrounds. Some have had experience in community
theatre, children's theatre, university theatre and high school theatre. Some have competed in University Interscholastic League
competitions in interpretation, prose, poetry, debate and drama.
None have had professional training or professional experience. The
students range in age from 18 to 30 and include freshmen, juniors
and seniors in college. Only two of these students intend to pursue
a full-time theatrical career. All stated that they greatly benefited by
using the steps of the Ten Line Exercise.

Sample Student Word Study No. 1

Character: Rosie Roberts
Play: *Spoon River Anthology*
Playwright: Edgar Lee Masters

Irish	died of old age
guilty	put down
defiant	quick temper
proud	high minded
not sorry	prostitute
killer	politically aware
cat	short hair
popular	curly hair
self defiance	no freckles
lesbian	large hips
angry	thick hair

didn't finish high school
bright
sharp
true
red head
buxom
brothel
have home to care for parents
righteous
long legs
alabaster
lace
satin
pillow talk
feathers
ruffles
sneered at
tired
hurt
penance
in love

small waist
small feet
long nails
taken advantage of
alcohol
cigarette
cigarette holder
Catholic
trustworthy
green
feminist
wants jail
not respected
put down
abortion
without incident
old
period
but not repeatedly
quick temper
Blaze Starr

This student wrote her word list in a cluster format with certain words circled and tied to other words which related in idea or theme.

Sample Student Sound Study No. 1

Character: Rosie Roberts
Play: *Spoon River Anthology*
Playwright: Edgar Lee Masters

a long audible sigh. . .
then the sound of someone taking a long, deep drag of a
    cigarette. . .
a woman's deep, throaty laughter.

the sharp sound of stiletto heels (or wooden sole shoes) on
    a wooden floor,

Fig. 20. Student visual study for Rosie Roberts.

suddenly the breaking of glass, like the shattering of a
  beer bottle against the floor.

quiet crying grows into moaning. . .
the moaning grows into screaming (the voice is powerful)
then the sounds of a woman cursing under her breath (the
  words are bitter but indiscernible).

Sample Student Visual Study No. 1

Character: Rosie Roberts
Play: *Spoon River Anthology*
Playwright: Edgar Lee Masters

Object: open red rose
(satin, silky, petals, blossomed, thorns, blood, beautiful)

I had received a dozen red roses on Friday and had begun to dry them late Friday night. On Sunday, I discovered that Rosie was most definitely best represented by an open, blood-red rose. I kept one of the roses out and put it in a vase. Last night I realized that the rose was too limp to blossom completely by itself, so I gently opened each petal manually. As I was doing that I felt overcome by the rightness, from a "Rosie" point of view, of the action. It symbolized, for me, Rosie's exploitation sexually as a brothel member.

I had left the rose hanging to dry just long enough that it stood straight by itself.

I was mesmerized by the soft silkiness of the petals.

Sample Student Movement Study No. 1

Character: Rosie Roberts
Play: *Spoon River Anthology*
Playwright: Edgar Lee Masters

Rosie walks freely, languidly with pelvis pushed forward and wide swinging of the hips...

She walks deliberately. She is aware of her breasts...

She holds her chest up high, shoulders back to accent her form.

She stops for a moment and lights a cigarette (using a long black cigarette holder) from which she takes long, deep drags. Her head is held high and tilted to the right. She licks her lips sensuously after each drag. She lets the smoke out of her mouth in a long, slow stream, almost hissing as she does.

She stamps out the cigarette and sits in a chair. She sighs audibly and crosses her arms across her chest with hands dangling over her knees.

She tries to move but, as though in molasses, she can't get out of her chair. She struggles to her feet and suddenly she stops and looks out into the audience . . .

She takes out another cigarette, lights it and puts her right foot up on the seat of the chair. She smiles and leans on her right knee . . .

"In my room, I shot him." She takes a long drag of the cigarette and throws her head back and laughs out loud. She strokes the side of her left thigh and looks at the audience in a daring manner.

She kicks over the chair and walks upstage into the shadows.

Sample Student Choice Study No. 1

Character: Rosie Roberts
Play: *Spoon River Anthology*
Playwright: Edgar Lee Masters

For character work on Rosie Roberts this student worked on an Irish accent and learned to sing burlesque-type songs. This helped her in developing the bawdy entertainer inherent in the character. She also worked in costume with high lace-up shoes, tight fitting bodice, ruffled skirts and low neckline dresses.

Sample Student Ten Line Study No. 1

Character: Rosie Roberts
Play: *Spoon River Anthology*
Playwright: Edgar Lee Masters

Rosie walks freely, her pelvis pushed forward, her hips swinging wide . . .
"I was sick, mad."
She lights a cigarette from a long black cigarette holder and takes a long deep drag.
" . . . gradually wasting away . . ."
She takes another drag and tilts her head back and to the right.

"I killed the son. . ."
> *She sits in a chair and crosses her arms over her chest, crosses her legs and dangles her hands over her knees. She drops the cigarette and stamps it out.*

". . .papers said he killed himself. . ."
> *She moves as though in molasses and struggles to get out of the chair.*

". . .the bribe of advertising. . ."
> *She struggles to overcome the force that holds her in her chair. Then suddenly she is free. She stands, looks at the audience and places her right foot up on the seat of the chair. She lets out a big laugh.*

"In my room I shot him."
> *She rubs her left thigh slightly lifting her skirt up to her knee.*

"He knocked me down. . ."
> *She stands on her two feet and laughs at the audience. Then she turns to go.*

"In spite of all the money I'd see my lover. . ."
> *She walks into the shadows.*

Sample Student Word Study No. 2

Character: Faith Matheny
Play: *Spoon River Anthology*
Playwright: Edgar Lee Masters

knowing smile	blue water
gliding	glowing
transcendent	elliptical
three	undulating
silver thread	royal couple
languid	repose
bridge	flowing
numinous	manna
moonlight on water	nirvana
lark	alabaster
auburn hair	bloom
muse	seer

Sample Student Sound Study No. 2

Character: Faith Matheny
Play: *Spoon River Anthology*
Playwright: Edgar Lee Masters

> ...the sound of distant thunder is repeated over and over again...
> ...the sound of thunder slowly fades and a rolling wave washing ashore is heard.
> ...a low, resonant hum is heard. It is the voice of Faith Matheny humming, low and soft.

Sample Student Visual Study No. 2

Character: Faith Matheny
Play: *Spoon River Anthology*
Playwright: Edgar Lee Masters

object: drawing

Although Faith is an aged and wise woman I chose to depict her as ageless and beautiful. I saw her standing in the wind, with hair flowing against an endless horizon. Her wisdom projects her through the ages and as she speaks of love, mystery, eternity and God she becomes a talisman for young people with hopes and dreams for the future. In this simple drawing I hoped to capture all these qualities.

Sample Student Movement Study No. 2

Character: Faith Matheny
Play: *Spoon River Anthology*
Playwright: Edgar Lee Masters

> the study begins with walking, almost floating steps...
> Faith walks back and forth with her arms making gliding movements...

Fig. 21. Student visual study for Faith Matheny.

the gliding movements slowly take on larger, swaying
movements. The subtle swaying gets larger, faster
and more energetic.
slowly she stops and outstretches her arms, palms
upturned...
her arms lift until they are over her head and she
looks up longingly.

Sample Student Choice Study No. 2

Character: Faith Matheny
Play: *Spoon River Anthology*
Playwright: Edgar Lee Masters

The choice exercise for this character involved the preparation of a family album complete with old pictures, pieces of fabric and lace, locks of hair and other memorabilia from Faith Matheny's family. The student found items for the album from her own family records and from local shops which carry old picture frames, linen doilies and pictures from the 1880s.

Sample Student Ten Line Study No. 2

Character: Faith Matheny
Play: *Spoon River Anthology*
Playwright: Edgar Lee Masters

Faith begins moving with slow, soft steps.
"At first you will not know what they mean, these sudden flashes in your soul, at midnight when the moon is full."
She walks slowly back and forth from right to left. She moves her arms in a gliding movement and slowly begins to sway her body, then her arms.
"A silence falls on speech, and his eyes without a flicker glow at you."
She becomes still and slowly drops her arms to her side. She slowly stretches her arms out in front of her, then opening them to the side, palms upturned.
"You two have seen the secret together, he sees it in you, and you in him, be brave, all souls who have such visions!"
With arms outstretched she walks forward and slowly lifts her arms over her head saying,
"You're catching a little whiff of the ether reserved for God himself."

Sample Student Word Study No. 3

Character: Harry Wilmans
Play: *Spoon River Anthology*
Playwright: Edgar Lee Masters

sorrow
compassion
humanity
void
no reconciliation
no atonement
no forgiveness
death
pestilence
death in life
snakes
will man do it again
hate
flag
patriotism
full of syphilis
disillusioned
stars in his eyes
gutted
not allowed to die

camaraderie
base humanity
suffering
hope
scream
voice
realization
awareness
visions
alive in death
Philippines
angry
denegration
pride
racism
stars and stripes
to spite my father
he cheered
a walking spirit
family connection

Sample Student Sound Study No. 3

Character: Harry Wilmans
Play: *Spoon River Anthology*
Playwright: Edgar Lee Masters

the sound of breathing, at first gentle breathing then
more anxious and heavy . . .
the sound of footsteps in the woods (twigs and branches
breaking and dry leaves crunching).
suddenly the sound of rifle fire in the distance.

Fig. 22. Student visual study for Harry Wilmans.

the footsteps turn into the sound of running and the
    breathing is deep and tense...
another round of gunfire and the sound of someone being
    shot...
he cries out in pain and begins to cry softly...
the breathing becomes labored and finally quiet...
the sound of Taps playing in the distance...

Sample Student Visual Study No. 3

Character: Harry Wilmans
Play: *Spoon River Anthology*
Playwright: Edgar Lee Masters

object: collage

There are various visual elements which represent Harry Wilmans so I chose to use a collage to best express this character.

I chose an old, faded and tattered American flag as the central focus for my visual study since war is the central theme for the character. I also used old photographs from the war period of the Spanish-American War in the late 1890s to show the horror and futility of the war experience.

I wanted my collage to resemble an 1890s *Guernica* because that painting is so powerful in its anti-war theme. Harry's life is ultimately summed up by the devastating effects of war, any war.

Sample Student Movement Study No. 3

Character: Harry Wilmans
Play: *Spoon River Anthology*
Playwright: Edgar Lee Masters

The character marches out facing the audience and salutes sharply...
He begins to look around suspiciously and he aims his rifle looking for the enemy...
Quickly he crouches down, his rifle drawn to fire...
His breathing becomes more audible and he is obviously frightened...
He hears the enemy in the distance and he rushes from left to right looking for something to shoot...
He tears off his cap in frustration and finally he sits down at the foot of a tree and buries his head in his folded arms...
He hears rifle fire and he slowly rises...
He is shot in the gut, he yells out in pain and falls to the ground...
He begins to cry shaking his head "No."

Sample Student Choice Study No. 3

Character: Harry Wilmans
Play: *Spoon River Anthology*
Playwright: Edgar Lee Masters

The student working on the character Harry Wilmans viewed the television program *The Civil War* by Ken Burns and subsequently did research on the book of the same title. The graphic pictures and poignant letters gave him a better understanding of the true horrors of war even though the character fought in the Spanish-American War in 1898.

Sample Student Ten Line Study No. 3

Character: Harry Wilmans
Play: *Spoon River Anthology*
Playwright: Edgar Lee Masters

I went to the war in spite of my father.

And followed the flag until I saw it raised—

The deadly water, and the cruel heat
and the smell of the trench

beastly acts   ourselves or alone

days of loathing and nights of fear

following the flag

I fell, with a scream, shot . . .

Sample Student Word Study No. 4

Character: Amanda Wingfield
Play: *The Glass Menagerie*
Playwright: Tennessee Williams

young   stubborn   willful   controlling   weak
controls because she's weak   pretty   debutante
charming   DENIAL   heartbroken   past
bad cook   useless   fearful   cheery appearance
masked   blind   selfish   feminine
feminine wiles   crafty   overly optimistic
blind because of denial   irrational
mother   overprotective   loving   hypocrite
quick to anger

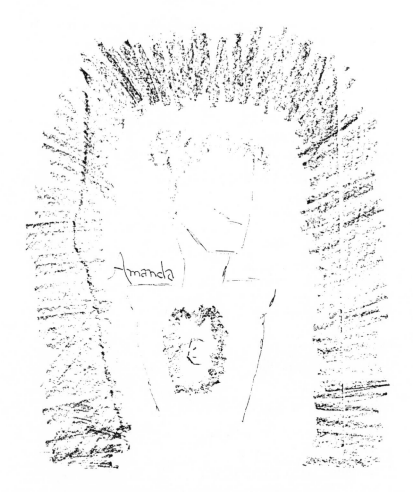

Fig. 23. Student visual study for Amanda Wingfield.

Sample Student Sound Study No. 4

Character: Amanda Wingfield
Play: *The Glass Menagerie*
Playwright: Tennessee Williams

the desperate silence of the room echoes the outside sounds. . .
the hum of motors outside, angry car horns, children playing in

the streets ... an irate neighbor yells at the children ... screeching protests from an alley cat ...

the sounds of a busy kitchen at home, running water, clanging silver ware as it is set on the table, tea kettle coming to a boil and whistling, stew boiling—"glub-plob, glub-glop" ...

the sound of nervous fingers drumming on the counter top (not the sound of a woman with long fingernails but a woman with short stubby fingernails).

the sound of stirring the stew, a cake ... feather duster, "swish, swish," accompanied by the sound of a woman humming a pleasant tune ... the sound of sweeping followed by cheery laughter ...

the rustling sound of bedsheets ... the creaking of an old bed, the tossing and turning of someone in bed who cannot sleep ...

the sound of someone sobbing quietly in their sleep ...

the pleasant sound of someone's voice with a melodious Southern accent saying, "old stories, old stories."

Sample Student Visual Study No. 4
Character: Amanda Wingfield
Play: *The Glass Menagerie*
Playwright: Tennessee Williams
object: drawing

I have long been fascinated by rubbings of gravestones, names at the Vietnam Memorial and objects from nature. I chose to express Amanda Wingfield visually by a rubbing which looks like it might have been taken from a cameo, since Amanda is interested in classic beauty. However, I chose to keep her facial features obscure. Rather, I drew her shoulders and jawline in a strong angle which symbolized the rigid and acute side of her personality.

Sample Student Movement Study No. 4
Character: Amanda Wingfield
Play: *The Glass Menagerie*
Playwright: Tennessee Williams

(The movement study for this character is composed of a series of gestures and movements.)

Wringing hands, drumming fingers, a rigid and upright posture (head high, chest out and buttocks tucked under), a walk that glides (she could walk with a book on her head), she is delicate yet has an imposing figure, a smile that is plastered on her face, batting eyelashes in front of all males, constantly in motion, keeps busy with small hand gestures, plays with her hair to keep it in place, wipes the corner of her mouth with her index finger careful not to smudge her lipstick.

Sample Student Choice Study No. 4

Character: Amanda Wingfield
Play: *The Glass Menagerie*
Playwright: Tennessee Williams

The character work for this character consisted of further study in the movement exercise. The student composed a movement study which included dance movements (which might be done at a cotillion), curtsies, and genteel gestures. These movements were then contrasted with household chores—mopping, sweeping, and washing dishes. The movement study finished with abstract movements expressing the lost dreams of the inner character.

Sample Student Ten Line Study No. 4

Character: Amanda Wingfield
Play: *The Glass Menagerie*
Playwright: Tennessee Williams

Amanda stands facing front, arms wide. She is full of excitement with exuberant gestures.
"Invitations poured in—parties all over the Delta! 'Stay in bed,' said Mother, 'you have a fever!'—but I just wouldn't. Evenings, dances! Afternoons of long, long rides! Picnics—lovely . . . I made the young men help me gather jonquils."
Amanda moves stage left and becomes relaxed and quiet. She nervously wrings her hands.

"That innocent look your father had everyone fooled! He smiled—
the world was enchanted! No girl can do worse that put herself at
the mercy of a handsome appearance!"

*Amanda becomes slumped in posture. Her face is tense and she
plays nervously with her hair.*

"I married a man who worked for the telephone company. A
telephone man who fell in love with long distance. Now he travels
and I don't even know where! But what I am going on for about
my—tribulations?"

*Amanda becomes more and more nervous. Her gestures are er-
ratic and she holds her hands with fingers wide apart and
strained.*

"Human beings are supposed to chew their food before they swallow
it down. Eat food leisurely, son, and really enjoy it. A well cooked
meal has lots of delicious flavors that have to be held in the mouth
for appreciation."

*Amanda leans forward on the back of a chair. Her voice becomes
forceful with undertones of anger.*

"What right have you got to jeopardize your job? Jeopardize the
security of us all? How do you think we'd manage if you were—"

Amanda raises her hands in frustration, hiding half of her face.

"We won't have a business career—we've given that up because it
gave us nervous indigestion. What is left but dependency all our
lives?"

Amanda looks off stage left, her voice full of false hope.

"Stay fresh and pretty! It's almost time for our gentlemen callers to
start arriving. How many do you suppose we're going to entertain
this afternoon? What? No one? You must be joking!"

Sample Student Word Study No. 5

Character: Biff Loman
Play: *Death of a Salesman*
Playwright: Arthur Miller

(This word list is composed in a cluster formation with the name
Biff Loman at the center.)

searching
niche
dreamer
realist

outdoor work
no boss
time to himself

lonely
popular
well-liked

handsome-tall
athletic
manual labor
can't live in city
no more masks

not good enough
let go, let go

confused
hurt
angry
betrayed

father's boy
likes masks
gray hair

fame and glory
name for himself
important
power

accepting limitations
thinking
jail
open spaces
well-liked

thief
proof of self worth
drifter
ranch

nothing
unforgiving
hateful

hurts himself
sporting goods
eager to please
childish

Sample Student Sound Study No. 5

Character: Biff Loman
Play: *Death of a Salesman*
Playwright: Arthur Miller

the study opens with the sound of someone whistling a happy
    tune...
while the whistling continues someone says, "Gee," then sound of
    someone catching a football. The football is thrown
    numerous times; each time the sound of exhalation of breath
    is louder and more effortful. The sound of someone's hands
    catching the football makes a loud "slap."
suddenly, there is the sound of horses galloping followed by an
    audible sigh...
then there is the sound of a hammer striking a nail into wood...

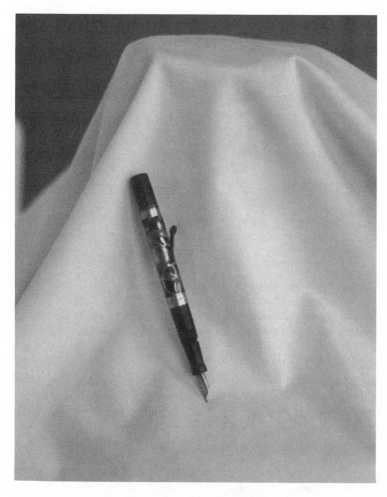

Fig. 24. Student visual for Biff Loman.

the hammering becomes louder and the sound of breathing gets
    louder. . .
suddenly the hammering stops and the sound of a cell door slam-
    ming closed is heard. . .
then there is the sound of a high-pitched, girlish giggling. . .
it is repeated over and over again. . .
"hmmm" followed by the inhalation and long exhalation of some-
    one smoking a cigarette. . .

the sound of a high school band playing a "fight song" plays softly as
    though someone is remembering another time...
cacophony, the sound of a car crash...
champagne bottles being opened, the sound of the cork popping
    then...
a man crying, sobbing softly, then completely...

Sample Student Visual Study No. 5

Character: Biff Loman
Play: *Death of a Salesman*
Playwright: Arthur Miller

object: photograph of a writing pen

The turning point in *Death of a Salesman* for Biff Loman is the
stealing of the pen from Bill Oliver's office. This theft represents, for
Biff, a turning point in which he not only matures, but is able to accept the transgressions of his father's past and those of his own life
as well. I tried to imagine a pen so expensive, so exquisite, that my
character, Biff, couldn't resist stealing it in order to impress his
father and to remind himself that he had been "somebody" in Bill
Oliver's office, too. I photographed the pen in many different positions and finally came up with the one shot that showed the pen in
an illusive and yet obtainable picture.

Sample Student Movement Study No. 5

Character: Biff Loman
Play: *Death of a Salesman*
Playwright: Arthur Miller

Biff is athletic but contained. Every movement is fluid and
physical.
    Standing with hands on hips, his back straight, head high, he is
smiling.
    The smile turns to a frown slowly, expressing irritation.

He becomes angry, still standing with hands on hips but now his chest and head fall forward. His face is firm, controlling fury.

His right hand comes out, palm up, raising it as if to ask a question. His face is impatient, waiting for an answer.

His head drops and hangs loosely. His left hand falls to his side, eyes closed, shoulders slumped. He has an expression of defeat.

Now his hands are up in front, pleading. He turns and picks up a clipboard and begins checking things off a list as he inspects items on a shelf. He is in earnest at first, his body alert, his eyes concentrating.

His concentration is replaced with boredom, then impatience. He throws the clipboard down and takes off his shirt.

He moves to one side and begins making shoveling motions. His face is set but content.

Sample Student Choice Study No. 5

Character: Biff Loman
Play: *Death of a Salesman*
Playwright: Arthur Miller

This student's choice exercise consisted of further investigation of the character through movement. He explored strong work efforts in order to experience the love of labor which Biff often expresses.

Sample Student Ten Line Study No. 5

Character: Biff Loman
Play: *Death of a Salesman*
Playwright: Arthur Miller

Biff stands with his hands on hips, back straight, head high and smiling.
"To suffer fifty weeks of the year for the sake of a two week vacation when all you really desire is to be outdoors, with your shirt off."
His face turns to a frown expressing irritation.

"I've always made a point of not wasting my life, and everytime I come back here I knew that all I've done is waste my life."

His right hand comes up, palm up, raising as if to ask a question. His face is impatient, waiting for an answer.

"I can't take hold of some kind of life."

He drops his head. His left hand falls to his side. His eyes are closed, his shoulders slumped.

"Screw the business world."

Now his hands are up, pleading.

"I was a shipping clerk."

His hands drop and he looks at someone in front of him.

"Dad, I'll make good, I'll make good."

He turns his head.

"I'm no good. can't you see what I am?"

He turns and picks up a clipboard and begins checking things off a list. He slowly becomes bored then impatient. He throws the clipboard and takes off his shirt.

"I stole a suit in Kansas City and I was in jail."

"And I never got anywhere because you blew me so full of hot air I could never take orders from anybody!"

He begins making shoveling motions.

"Pop, I'm nothing."

His face is set but content.

To some, growth is almost all memory and recollection. . . .

To some, growth lies in learning how gadgets work . . . to develop a new method but to become extremely adept at the old one.

To some, growth is the extension of ready-made faith. It sets the follower apart and makes him superior to the common herd. . . . He . . . becomes a pseudo artist. . . .

To some few, growth is the discovery of a dynamic power of the mind. There is a long period of intense study, criticism, and self-examination. . . . The growth is precious and very private. . . . This mind is at home in any period, in any place where genius has produced lasting works.

—PAUL BAKER

VI

THE ACTOR AT WORK

Paul Baker has taught thousands of students who have passed through his classes at Baylor University and Trinity University to work for their own unique discovery. His teaching went against most traditional approaches to the art of the theatre because he was and is interested in working for discovery rather than for results.

The exercises found in this book are developed for the actor working for a discovery of his own self and his own interpretation of the dramatic character. Many directors will ask for quick results. Many teachers will try to impose a characterization on the actor. The actor's task is to take creative risks and resist the temptation to imitate or find the easiest and faster route to a finished performance.

The studies that make up the Ten Line Exercise can be used while the actor prepares for an audition, with or without the aid of a dramatic coach or teacher. They enable the actor to pursue his own character in his own manner, striving for a truly unique and fresh presentation of the character within the context of the play. He may also use these studies in preparation for an audition with the aid of coach or teacher. The objective eye of the teacher can help the actor to understand what he is communicating in his presentation. This valuable information can help in honing, reshaping and refining the characterization.

These studies can be especially useful in a classroom situation. If all of the student actors in a class are investigating each of the studies at their own pace and with varying results, the growth of the class as a whole will be enhanced. Fellow classmates as well as the instructor can provide numerous objective accounts of how the character is being portrayed. All must be reminded that this is work in progress and judgments must be based on what is being communicated and how by the student actor; one must not impose a right vs. wrong judgment on the work.

Students learn how to approach the various studies by observing other students' work. Some student actors work best through movement, others through visual or auditory means. Some students can work more abstractly while others are bound by a literal and conventional approach.

Through the past few years I have found through my own work and from the work of my students that these studies are most beneficial when used in conjunction with rehearsals for performance. Many directors may lack the time or inclination to do improvisational work or experimentation as part of rehearsal periods. When and if this occurs the actor has at his disposal a series of studies which provide an opportunity to investigate the character on his own. Both the director and the actor can find that rehearsal sessions go more quickly and progress more steadily when the actor is prepared to investigate the character on his own.

Oftentimes the director is looking at the production as a whole. He has obligations to check with the scene designer, the lighting designer, the costume designer, and the prop, sound, makeup and art designers. His interests are in the blocking of each scene, keeping within the budget for the show and making the whole production come together on time. He may not have the skills to help an actor investigate his part. If the role is a minor one, one without many lines of dialogue or without critical action, he may spend very little time at all helping the actor find his role. Robert Barton describes three types of directors in his book *Acting: Onstage and Off.*

> An acting *teacher* creates an environment (physical and emotional) and provides exercises, to help you explore and discover your own potential. . . .

An acting *coach* functions much like a coach in sports, working with you on specific problems, having you try a number of solutions. . . .

A *director* is the most likely of the three to impose his will on yours. He is the most likely to tell you . . . exactly what he wants. . . .[51]

Some directors will tell you exactly what they want without any clue as to how you can achieve it. Other directors will tell you exactly what they want and rigidly impose on you the ways and means to achieve it. This is not collaboration and it does not foster a creative and supportive atmosphere in rehearsals or performance.

Some directors never tell you, at least in terms you can understand, what they want from you or your character. You are left out on your own, and the method you use to prepare the role is of your own choosing. Many actors don't know where to begin unless the director tells them "Do this," "Don't do that," or "Why can't you play it this way?"

The actor must learn to rely on his own devices and his own methods of personal research to find the character. If you have a truly collaborative, supportive and sensitive director who is willing to take the time and has the improvisational skills to help you and other members of the cast to investigate their role, then consider yourself lucky. Very, very lucky.

The Ten Line Exercise is vital to the actor who plays a minor role. He too must find the essence of the character. He too must develop a believable, fresh and unique character even though he may be onstage for only a few moments. These studies provide creative, in-depth character investigation.

Finally, the Ten Line Exercise can be useful for the actor in performance. Imagine you are playing a role in a regional repertory company, Off Broadway or on Broadway. You may have eight performances a week. How can you keep the character fresh? How can you keep the illusion of the "first time" or first performance about your character? How can you cry or laugh or rise to a high level of passion on cue every night for eight performances a week, for weeks or months of the run of a play?

It is difficult to accomplish repeat performances with the same freshness and originality as on opening night. If you find that your performance is becoming old or tired, or it feels as though you are just walking through the part, try repeating one of the studies you did in your initial investigation of the role.

Repeating the movement study or re-examining the sound study can get you into a new outlook on the character. Going through the movement study or the ten line study as part of your warm-up before performance is beneficial, too.

The Actor at Work Alone

As you prepare for an audition, for class work, for rehearsal or for performance, you will no doubt learn how you learn. You may discover that you learn by reading and doing research or by relating to visual images that are associated with the character or with the play as a whole. You may discover that you need to bounce ideas off of other actors in a group setting. Whatever you discover about yourself will provide valuable information that you can use in the future.

Seek to discover your own working methods. Seek to understand how and when and where you work best. You may not always be able to control the when or the why or the how, but you will have analyzed and evaluated the methods which work best for you, and that is more than many actors know about their craft.

Two ways of enhancing your self-discovery and charting your progress as an actor are to develop discipline and to keep a journal. You may think that discipline, like talent, is something you are born with, not something that you can develop. This is not true. Progress of any kind is largely dependent on the discipline you impose on yourself.

Discipline does not restrict you; rather it frees you. It is your self-discipline that enables you to take creative risks. It helps you to work within a field that is not only highly competitive, but highly guided by rules as well.

Producers and directors of today are interested in actors that can meet the deadlines and stress-related expectations of this rigorous lifestyle. Actors must be punctual, prepared, alert and selfless. The actor who makes his own rules — who arrives late or un-prepared for a day's work, who is haughty or selfish in his approach to ensemble work, who doesn't know his lines or remember his blocking — is definitely the exception today. The competition is too stiff. There is no room for an actor who can't work, doesn't know how to work or is too undisciplined to work.

Mira Felner explains in her book *Free to Act;*

> Being prepared is essential to maintaining the creative flow. When you work with others, it is upsetting if a scene partner has not studied the material or is consistently late to rehearsal. Antagonism and anxiety engendered by an uncaring actor can stymie the creative process. If you cannot count on your partners to be there, ready and committed, it is impossible to trust them with your feelings. Actors have a special obligation to be responsible to each other and to their work.[52]

A journal which is specific to work in progress in acting is especially beneficial to the actor who wishes to understand his working methods and his advancement from one role to the next. Consider keeping a journal in class, in rehearsal and in performance. Pay particular attention to feelings, insights, questions about your work or working methods, images and perceptions. Remember that a journal records experiences and provides insight. It should not be a place for self-doubts, self-criticism, or the accounts of others' criticism toward your work.

Christina Baldwin in her book *One to One: Self-Understanding Through Journal Writing* says that "The journal is a way of connecting. The journal is a connection of the self with the self. . . . It becomes a way of observing survival. It becomes an instrument of survival."[53] Baldwin suggests using "flow writing" because it is the least restrictive in style. The stream of consciousness style of writing allows you to write without attention to grammar, punctuation or spelling. It is free association and can surprise you with ideas you were not aware of consciously.

At some point in your journal writing it is important to address specific concerns relating to acting and performing. Since journal writing is a solitary act it can give you an opportunity to explore people, places and events of your past as well as your present. Consider that memories of your childhood can be used in the development of your character.

Stanislavski's Magic If and Sense Memory exercises are based on images, perceptions and speculations we have about our past. The journal gives you an excellent manner in which to investigate your sense and emotion memories. You can analyze and evaluate them for use in preparation of your role.

Journal writing can also help you to work outside and beyond the scope of your own typecasting. If you are young and petite and soft-spoken, use your journal writing to record images of yourself in the role of someone who is aggressive, old, loud and imposing.

Sam Keen poses a variety of interesting and helpful exercises in his book *Your Mythic Journey: Finding Meaning in Your Life Through Writing and Storytelling.* He outlines much of his book in the chapters "The Present," "The Past" and "The Future." He then offers scenarios and a list of questions for consideration in each chapter. For example, in "The Public Self" he offers these questions;

> In what ways are you unique? What qualities distinguish you from your friends, your enemies, the masses? Do you think other people consider you unusual? Odd? Average? A character? An individual? Unobtrusive? Hostile? Do you agree with them?
>
> If you were placed suddenly in an alien culture how would you identify with and distinguish yourself from the natives?
>
> If you were to die tomorrow how much of the story of your life could be reconstructed from what other people know of you? Who knows you best? How much of your essential self is public and how much is private? How would you be remembered?[54]

Many of the "Viewpoints" and questions Keen uses in his book can be helpful in the process of self-discovery. These same examples can be turned around and asked of the character for an innovative and introspective view of the role.

Self-discipline, journal writing as a means to self-discovery and self-awareness, a sense of artistic integrity, and the dedication to pursue your own path are the primary elements anyone needs to become an actor.

Uta Hagen concludes her book *Respect for Acting* by stating, "Consistently good acting is never an accident. . . . To achieve a technique which will allow for a genuine existence on stage can take a lifetime to accomplish. The search never stops; there are no dead ends."[55]

The actor as artist must strive to achieve a sense of artistic integrity with his working methods and product. He accomplishes this goal by setting high standards for his creative work.

Paul Baker shared his definition of creative work with countless numbers of students. Baker says that creative work "is anything which has taken the work of your head, hands, heart or imagination. . . . Any one of four of these can be used. . . It must involve ideas of your own and you must have been completely concentrated. . . . Anything fresh out of you is creative work. . . ."[56]

A study of acting is a study of human responses to a variety of situations and circumstances. A study of acting does more than prepare us for a career in the theatre. It teaches us to be students of life while we become students of our own inner workings. We can become more sensitive and compassionate people through a study of acting.

Dramatic characters present a view of the human condition, and as we involve ourselves in the process of making theatre we begin to understand that there are a variety of ways in which humans respond to life's situations. As we begin to interpret our role we struggle to find a common ground on which to relate to and understand the character's motivations and feelings, and in doing so we experience empathy. Theatre is a mirror to life, and as students of theatre we gain a greater understanding of the possibilities of human interaction through the interpretation of dramatic characters.

At the heart of interpretative work is creative work. A creative state of mind allows not only self-discovery but insight into the creative work of others as well. This is especially true in the arts: painters can learn from dancers, poets learn from sculptors, and musicians learn from actors.

The creative artist follows five levels of knowledge in his pursuit of a level of maturity and excellence. Theatre practitioner Mary Lou Hoyle outlined these five levels of creative knowledge at the Second Harvest, a recent conference honoring Paul Baker.

First is self-knowledge. This type of self-knowledge is as the Greeks intended. They believed in a firm understanding of one's spiritual, physical and intellectual selves. Know your limits, know your strengths and above all know your potential.

Second is knowledge of your space. In particular, know your working space. How do you get work accomplished? How do you work with others? What are your creative barriers? What are your blocks? If you have knowledge of your working limits and barriers, it will be easier to overcome them. Spend time in investigating different modes or styles of working. Experiment with different media. Find out what works for you and try to eliminate what doesn't work.

Third is knowledge of all arts. True creative, artistic knowledge is not limited to an exclusive study of your particular interest. All of the arts are interrelated. Develop a knowledge of painting, sculpture, choreography, dance, rhythm in music, creative writing, poetry, design and acting. Your knowledge of one art will enhance the understanding of the other. Remember that you are discovering what is there, what is represented or communicated in the art. You are seeking to discover more about who you are and how you relate to all the arts. Avoid trying to find your slot or niche.

Fourth is knowledge from a master. The benefits of studying with a master teacher or master artist are especially important to your own growth as an artist. This may involve apprenticeship work, internship work or time spent as a journeyman in training. At this point of your creative work you can begin to narrow your focus and hone your skills. You now have knowledge of self, working methods and the interrelatedness of the arts, all of which serve to bolster your spirit and prepare you for intensive training with an accomplished and experienced master artist.

Fifth is knowledge of teaching. This final and highest level of knowledge is attainable only after completion of the previous levels. You may not become a teacher by trade, but you can pass on what knowledge and experience have given you. The ability to share your skills, knowledge and unique point of view can be your highest gift. As a teacher you can further the study of knowledge by sharing what you have learned and in that sharing you gain further knowledge yourself. This type of teaching is a compassionate and selfless act. It demonstrates a willingness to give, to share, to learn and to further your ideas.

The actor in his work with other actors who may be a part of a class or a cast ultimately finds himself in a lonely position. He interacts, responds, reacts and involves himself with others in preparation and performance, yet he ultimately is alone in his perceptions of himself and the process of acting. His work always begins and ends with his body, his mind and his intellect, all three the expressive components of the art to which he seeks to create.

APPENDIX

The following is a partial list of institutions offering degree-granting and non–degree-granting programs in theatre. All of these institutions have membership with the National Association of Schools of Theatre.

American Academy of Dramatic
  Arts
120 Madison Avenue
New York, NY 10016

American Academy of Dramatic
  Arts — West
2550 Paloma Street
Pasadena, CA 91107

Auburn University
A. Cleveland Harrison
Department of Theatre
Auburn University, AL
  36849-5422

Brigham Young University
Department of Theatre
Division of Fine Arts
Provo, UT 84602

California State University at Fresno
5241 N. Maple
Fresno, California 93740-0048

Dartmouth College
Lewis Crickard
Department of Drama and Film
  Studies
Hinman 6204 Hopkins Center
Hanover, NH 03755

Howard University
Carole W. Singleton
Department of Drama
6th and Fairmont Sts. N. W.
Washington, D. C. 20059-0001

Indiana University at Bloomington
Bryan Hall
Bloomington, IN 47405

University of Massachusetts at
  Amherst
Roberta Uno Thelwell
New World Theater
Box 63 Student Union
Amherst, MA 01003

University of Miami
Robert Ankrom
Department of Theatre Arts
P. O. Box 248273
University Station
Coral Gables, FL 33124

Michigan State University
John Baldwin
Department of Theatre
149 Auditorium
East Lansing, MI 48824-1046

University of New Mexico
James Linnell
Department of Theatre Arts
Fine Arts Center Room 1412
Albuquerque, NM 87131

Northwestern University
633 Clark Street
Evanston, IL 60208

University of Texas at Austin
Coleman Jennings
Department of Drama, Win. 1.142
Austin, TX 78712

University of Washington
Department of Theatre
Seattle, WA 98195

The following is a partial list of degree-granting and non–degree-granting programs in theatre. All of these institutions have membership in the Association for Theatre in Higher Educations.

Actors Movement Studio, Inc.
Lloyd A. Williamson
298 5th Ave.
P.O. Box 220
New York, NY 10001

Agnes Scott College
Becky B. Prophet
Department of Theatre
East College Ave.
Decatur, GA 30030

American Center for Stanislavski
  Theatre Art
Sonia Moore
285 Park Ave. #6A
New York, NY 10022

American Musical and Dramatic
  Academy

Judith Davis
Director of Education
2109 Broadway
New York, NY 10023

Audition Training Institute
Ginger Friedman
303 East 83rd St. #15-B
New York, NY 10028

Brandeis University
Michael Murray
Department of Theatre Arts
P.O. Box 9110
Waltham, MA 02254-9110

California Institute of the Arts
Ruben Sierra
School of Theatre
24700 McBean Parkway
Valencia, CA 91355

University of California at Irvine
Robert Cohen
School of Fine Arts — Drama
Irvine, CA 92717

Carnegie Mellon University
Shirley Woods
School of Urban and Public
    Affairs
Pittsburgh, PA 15213

University of Colorado at Boulder
James Symons
Department of Theatre and
    Dance Box 261
Boulder, CO 80309-0261

Eugene O'Neill Theater Center
Craig Winstead
National Theater Institute
305 Great Neck Road
Waterford, CT 06385

Florida State University
Gil Lazier
School of Theatre
Tallahassee, FL 32306-2008

Grinnell College
Ellen Mease
Department of Theatre
P.O. Box 805
Grinnell, IA 50112-0809

Hunter College
Mira Felner
Department of Theatre and Film
695 Park Ave. Rm. 336 HN
New York, NY 10021

National Shakespeare
    Conservatory
Diane L. Turnbull
591 Broadway 6th Floor
New York, NY 10012

National Theatre Conservatory
Tony Church
1050 13th St.
Denver, CO 80204

New York University
J. Michael Miller
Tisch School of the Arts
721 Broadway Room 719
New York, NY 10003

Oberlin College
William J. Byrnes
Department of Theatre and
    Dance
Warner Center
Oberlin, OH 44074

Southern Methodist University
Cecil O'Neal
Theatre Division
Owens Arts Center, Rm S-100
Dallas, TX 75275

Stanford University
Charles R. Lyons
Department of Drama
Memorial Auditorium, M144
Stanford, CA 94305-5010

Yale University
David DeRose
Theatre Studies Program
254 York Street
New Haven, CT 06520-2962

The following is a partial list of other degree-granting and non–degree-granting institutions offering programs in theatre.

University of California at Los
Angeles
Andrea L. Rich
School of Theatre, Film and
Television
405 Hilgard Ave.
Los Angeles, CA 90024

American Conservatory Theatre
Maureen McKibbon
450 Geary St.
San Francisco, CA 94102

American Film Institute — Center
for Advanced Film and Television Studies
Jean Firstenberg
2021 N Western Ave.
Los Angeles, CA 90027

Goodman School of Drama
DePaul University
804 West Belden
Chicago, IL 60614

The Juilliard School
Michael Langham
Lincoln Center
New York, NY 10023

NOTES

1. Paul Baker, speech given in 1941 and 1966. Excerpts appear in *The Paul Baker Theater: A Photo History,* Central Texas Printing, 1990.

2. *Ibid.*

3. Constantin Stanislavski, *An Actor's Handbook,* ed. and transl. by Elizabeth Reynolds Hapgood (New York: Theatre Arts Books, 1963), p. 11.

4. Peter Brook, *The Empty Space* (New York: Avon Books, 1968), p. 127.

5. *Ibid.,* p. 126.

6. Joel G. Fink, "Too, Too Solid Flesh" (Baltimore, Md: *Theatre Topics,* vol. 1, no. 2, September, 1991), p. 119.

7. Don Richardson, *Acting Without Agony* (Needham Heights, Mass.: Allyn and Bacon, 1988), p. 12.

8. Joseph Chaikin, *The Presence of the Actor* (New York: Atheneum, 1972), pp. 5–6.

9. Richardson, p. 12.

10. Brook, pp. 24–25.

11. Paul Baker, *Integration of Abilities: Exercises for Creative Growth* (San Antonio: Trinity University Press, 1972), p. viii.

12. *Ibid.,* Preface.

13. Interview with Sally Netzel, Dallas Theatre Center, January 21, 1975.

14. Michael Chekhov, *To the Actor* (New York: Harper and Row, 1953), p. 4.

15. Edward T. Hall, *The Hidden Dimension* (Garden City, NY: Anchor Books, 1969).

16. Doris Humphrey, *The Art of Making Dances*, edited by Barbara Pollack (New York: Grove Press, 1959), p. 104.

17. J. L. Styan, *The Elements of Drama* (Cambridge: Cambridge University Press, 1967), p. 141.

18. William Shakespeare, *Shakespeare: The Complete Works*, edited by G. B. Harrison (New York: Harcourt, Brace and World, 1968), p. 1199.

19. Oscar Wilde, *The Importance of Being Earnest* (New York: Samuel French), pp. 45–49.

20. Brook, p. 26.

21. Constantin Stanislavsky, *Constantin Stanislavski on the Art of the Stage*, transl. by David Magarshack (New York: Hill and Wang, 1961), p. 107.

22. Thornton Wilder, *Our Town* (New York: Coward-McCann, 1938), p. 36, Act I.

23. Baker, *Integration of Abilities: Exercises for Creative Growth*, p. 65.

24. *Ibid.*, p. 29.

25. Karl Shapiro, ed., *American Poetry* (New York: Thomas Y. Crowell, 1960), p. 85.

26. David Cole, *The Theatrical Event: A Mythos, a Vocabulary, a Perspective* (Middletown, Conn.: Wesleyan University Press, 1975), pp. 7–8.

27. Stanislavski, *An Actor's Handbook*, p. 55.

28. Ernestine Stodelle, *The Dance Technique of Doris Humphrey and Its Creative Potential* (Princeton, NJ: Princeton Book Company, 1978), p. 13.

29. Samuel Thornton, *Laban's Theory of Movement* (Boston: Play's Inc., 1971), p. 1.

30. Cecelia Dell, *A Primer for Movement Description* (New York: Dance Notation Bureau, 1970), p. 49.

31. *Ibid.*, p. 55.

32. Claudia Sullivan, *The Actor Moves* (Jefferson, NC: McFarland, 1990), p. 46.

33. Stanislavski, *An Actor's Handbook*, p. 9.

34. Baker, pp. 129–130.

35. Constantin Stanislavski, *Creating a Role* (New York: Theatre Arts Books, 1949), p. 62.

36. Baker, p. 149.

37. Stanislavski, transl. by Hapgood, p. 11.

38. Silvano Arieti, *Creativity: The Magic Synthesis* (New York: Basic Books, 1976), p. 339.

39. Interview with Sally Netzel, Dallas Theatre Center, January 21, 1975.

40. *Ibid.*

41. Michael Chekhov, *To the Actor* (New York: Harper and Row, 1953), p. 25.

42. Baker, *Integration of Abilities: Exercises for Creative Growth*, pp. 143–144.

43. Netzel interview.

44. Eliot D. Chapple and Martha Davis, "Expressive Movement and Performance: Towards a Unifying Theory," *Tulane Drama Review*, Winter 1988, p. 53.

45. Robinson Jeffers, *Not Man Apart*, ed. David Brower (New York: Ballantine Books, 1965), pp. 78–80.

46. Interview with Sally Netzel, Dallas Theatre Center, March 23, 1976.

47. *Ibid.*

48. *Ibid.*

49. Robert Edmond Jones, *The Dramatic Imagination* (New York: Theatre Arts Books, 1941), pp. 31–32.

50. Michael Chekhov, *To The Actor* (New York: Harper and Row, 1953), p. 17.

51. Robert Barton, *Acting: Onstage and Off* (New York: Holt, Rinehart and Winston, 1989), pp. 215–216.

52. Mira Felner, *Free to Act* (New York: Holt, Rinehart and Winston, 1990), p. 6.

53. Christina Baldwin, *One to One: Self-Understanding Through Journal Writing* (New York: M. Evans, 1977), p. xiv.

54. Sam Keen and Anne Valley-Fox, *Your Mythic Journey: Finding Meaning in Your Life Through Writing and Storytelling* (Los Angeles: Tarcher, 1989), p. 10.

55. Uta Hagen, *Respect for Acting* (New York: Macmillan, 1973), p. 222.

56. Paul Baker, interview on videotape, Second Harvest Conference honoring Paul Baker, Waco, Texas, August 1990.

BIBLIOGRAPHY

Acting

Abbott, Leslie. *Active Acting.* Belmont, Calif.: Star Publishing, 1987.

Barton Robert. *Acting: Onstage and Off.* New York: Holt, Rinehart and Winston, 1989.

Benedetti, Robert. *The Actor at Work.* Englewood Cliffs, N. J.: Prentice-Hall, 1981.

Boleslavsky, Richard. *Acting: The First Six Lessons.* New York: Theatre Arts Books, 1982.

Brook, Peter. *The Empty Space.* New York: Avon, 1968.

Camryn, Walter. *An Analytical Study of Character Movement for Dancers, Actors.* New York: Dance Mart, 1959.

Chaikin, Joseph. *The Presence of the Actor.* New York: Atheneum, 1972.

Chekhov, Michael. *To the Actor: on the Technique of Acting.* New York: Harper and Row, 1953.

Chinoy, Helen Krich, and Cole, Toby, eds. *Actors on Acting.* New York: Crown, 1970.

Cohen, Robert. *Acting in Shakespeare.* Mountain View, Calif.: Mayfield, 1991.

_____. *Acting One.* Mountain View, Calif.: Mayfield, 1984.

_____. *Acting Power.* Mountain View, Calif.: Mayfield, 1978.

_____. *Acting Professionally.* Palo Alto, Calif.: Mayfield, 1981.

Crawford, Jerry L. *Acting: In Person and In Style.* Dubuque, Iowa: Wm. C. Brown, 1983.

Delgado, Ramon. *Acting with Both Sides of Your Brain.* New York: Holt, Rinehart and Winston, 1986.

Diderot, Denis. *The Paradox of Acting* [1773]. New York: Hill and Wang, 1957.

Edwards, Christine. *The Stanislavski Heritage.* New York: New York University Press, 1965.

Felner, Mira. *Free to Act.* New York: Holt, Rinehart and Winston, 1990.

Fishman, Morris. *The Actor in Training.* Westport, Conn.: Greenwood, 1961.

Grotowski, Jerzy. *Towards a Poor Theatre.* New York: Simon and Schuster, 1968.

Hagen, Uta. *Respect for Acting.* New York: Macmillan, 1973.

Hethmon, Robert, ed. *Strasberg at the Actor's Studio.* New York: Viking, 1965.

Joseph, Bertram. *Acting Shakespeare.* New York: Theatre Arts Books, 1969.

King, Nancy. *Theatre Movement: The Actor and His Space.* New York: Drama Books Specialists, 1971.

Marowitz, Charles. *The Act of Being: Towards a Theory of Acting.* New York: Taplinger, 1978.

Moore, Sonia. *The Stanislavski System: The Professional Training of an Actor.* New York: Pocket Books, 1951.

_____. *Stanislavski Today.* New York: New York Center for Stanislavski Theatre Art, 1973.

_____. *Training an Actor,* rev. ed. New York: Penguin Books, 1979.

Stanislavski, Constantin. *Building a Character,* transl. by Elizabeth Reynolds Hapgood. New York: Theatre Arts Books, 1949.

_____. *Creating a Role,* transl. by Elizabeth Reynolds Hapgood. New York: Theatre Arts Books, 1949.

_____. *My Life in Art,* transl. by J. J. Robbins. New York: Theatre Arts Books, 1948.

Performance Theory

Artraud, Antonin, *The Theatre and Its Double,* transl. by Mary Caroline Richards. New York: Grove Press, 1958.

Baker, Paul. *Integration of Abilities: Exercises for Creative Growth.* San Antonio, Texas: Trinity University Press, 1972.

Goldman, Michael. *Acting and Action in Shakespearean Tragedy.* Princeton, N.J.: Princeton University Press, 1958.

Movement for the Actor

Battye, Marguerite. *Stage Movement.* London: Herbert Jenkins, 1954.

Davis, Martha. *Understanding Body Movement.* New York: Arno Press, 1972.

Kline, Peter, and Meadows, Nancy. *The Theatre Student: Physical Movement for the Theatre.* New York: Richard Rosen Press, 1971.

Laban, Rudolf. *The Mastery of Movement,* ed. Lisa Ullmann. Boston: Plays, 1971.

Penrod, Joseph. *Movement for the Performing Artist.* Palo Alto, Calif.: Mayfield, 1974.

Pisk, Liz. *The Actor and His Body.* New York: Theatre Arts Books, 1975.

Rubin, Lucille S. *Movement for the Actor.* New York: Drama Books Specialists, 1980.

Sabatine, Jean. *The Actor's Image: Movement Training for Stage and Screen.* Coll. David Hodges. Englewood Cliffs, N.J.: Prentice-Hall, 1983.

Auditioning

Hung, Gordon. *How to Audition for TV, Movies, Commercials, Plays, Musicals.* New York: Harper and Row, 1977.

Shurtleff, Michael. *Audition.* New York: Bantam, 1980.

Journal Writing

Baldwin, Christina. *One to One: Self-Understanding Through Journal Writing.* New York: M. Evans and Company, 1977.

Goldberg, Natalie. *Writing Down the Bones.* Boston: Shambhala Publ., 1986.

Keen, Sam, and Valley-Fox, Anne. *Your Mythic Journey: Finding Meaning in Your Life Through Writing and Storytelling.* Los Angeles: Tarcher, Inc., 1989.

Progoff, Ira. *At a Journal Workshop.* New York: Dialogue House Library, 1975.

INDEX

abstract movement 67, 69
abstract sweeping movements 96
accent work 51
acting 10, 11, 12
Acting: Onstage and Off 144
acting coach 145
Acting Without Acting 13
Actor's Studio 18, 19
Adler, Stella 18
Appia, Adolphe 21
Arieti, Silvano 56
Artaud, Antonin xiii
artistic integrity 148
Arts Magnet School 20
As I Lay Dying 4
auditory rhythms 31

Baker, Paul v, xii, xiii, 1, 2, 3, 4,
  5, 20, 52, 62, 99, 143, 149
Baldwin, Christina 147
Braton, Robert 144
Bauhaus Group 21, 52
Baylor University xii, 1, 2, 3, 20,
  143

beauty 13
Beavers, Virgil 3
Benedetti, Robert 19
Benge, Sharon xii
Bissiere 2
body image 45
body movements 40
body tensions 105
Brando, Marlon 19
Brook, Peter 10, 11, 19

Casa Manana Theatre School xii
Chagall, Marc 2
Chaikin, Joseph 13, 19
character objectivity 68
character study 67
characterization 60, 143
Chekhov, Anton 11
Chekhov, Michael 22, 62, 107
The Christian Science Monitor 4
clichés 92
Clurman, Harold 18
Cole, David 37
collage 85, 87

Commedia dell'Arte 41
completeness 13
constructivism 75
Cook, Carole 3
"cookie cutter" style of acting 11,
    56
corps de danse 67
costumes 75
craft 11, 12, 13
craft of acting 12
Craig, Gordon 21
creation of a character 107
creative expression 2
creative philosophy 47

Dallas Theatre Center v, xii, xiii,
    3, 4, 20, 59, 99, 112
dance 67
Dance in America 39
dance work 51
Dean, James 19
Death of a Salesman 61, 64, 135,
    136, 138, 139
déjà vu 37
design 66
A Different Drummer 3
A Doll's House 67
dramatic analysis 73, 74
dramatic analysis, elements of:
    characterization 74, 75; form
    and spirit 74, 75; idea 74, 75;
    language and sound 74, 75; plot
    74; visual elements 74, 75
dramatic elements 101
Dramatic Imagination 107
dramatic impressions 27

effort actions 93
efforts 93; dab 93, 95; flick 93,
    94, 95; float 93, 94, 95; glide
    93, 94; press 93, 94; punch 93,
    94; slash 93, 95; wring 93, 94,
    95

Eightfold Path 98
elements of art: color and texture
    19, 20, 35, 47, 66, 90, 92; line
    and direction 19, 20, 43, 45, 47;
    movement 19, 20, 39, 47;
    rhythm 19, 20, 23, 24, 25, 27,
    32, 47, 67; silhouette 19, 20,
    45, 47, 87, 88; sound and
    silence 19, 20, 35, 47; space 19,
    20, 32, 33, 35, 47
The Elephant Man 57
Elizabethan 41
emotion memory 18, 38
emotional associations 92
emotional intensity 83
emotional levels 68
emotional quality 38
The Empty Space 10
energy level 38
environmental sounds 35
essential sounds 81
expressionism 43
external attitudes 101
external tension 92

Faulkner, William 4
Felner Mira
Fink, Joel G. 12
Flatt, Robyn v
flexibility 58
flow of movement 40
flow writing 147
fluency of thinking 58
Flynn, Robert 4
focusing 57
foreign language work 51
form 13
form of a performance 68
Four Noble Truths 98
Free to Act 147

gestures and mannerisms 45
The Ghost Sonata 76, 86, 98

The Glass Menagerie 35, 131, 132, 133, 134
Graham, Martha 39
Greek 12, 41, 51
Grotowski, Jerzy xiii, 18, 19
Gulager, Clu 3

habitual patterns 25
Hagen, Uta 19, 148
Hamlet 3
Hermann, Edward 3
horizontal plane 3
Hoyle, Mary Lou 149
human movement 93
Humphrey, Doris 24, 25, 39

Ibsen, Henrik 67
illud tempus 37
"the illusion of the first time" 58, 145
immersion 57
The Importance of Being Earnest 27, 28
improvisational style 40
individual expression 33
inner intention 45
integration philosophy 20

Jack Ruby: All-American Boy 99
Jeffers, Robinson 97
Jenkins, Paul 91
Jones, Mary Sue v
Jones, Preston 4
Jones, Robert Edmond 107
journal 146, 147
journal writing 148
Journey 41
Journey to Jefferson 4
Jung, Carl 9

Keen, Sam 148
Kennedy Center 4
kinetics 23
Klee, Paul 52

Laban, Rudolf 93; effort vocabulary 93
"Landscape" 2
The Last Meeting of the Knights of the White Magnolias 4
Laughton, Charles 3
The Life and Times of Joseph Stalin 99
Life magazine 4
lighting 75
Long Day's Journey into Night xii
Luann Hampton Overlander Laverty 4

Macbeth 27
McKinney, Eugene 3, 4
"magic if" 18, 147
Maholy-Nagy 21
mannerisms 66
Maslow, Abraham 55
Masters, Edgar Lee 119, 120, 122, 123, 124, 125, 127, 128, 129, 130, 131
mechanical sounds 36, 37
Meisner, Sanford 18, 19
mental spaces 33
Meredith, Burgess 3
"method of physical actions" 18, 50
Miller, Arthur 61, 135, 136, 138, 139
mind-body connection 51
Molière 67
Mondrian, Piet 3, 52
Moore, Randy 112
motifs 66
motion factors: flow 93; space 93; time 93; weight 93

motor rhythm 23
movement: directional movement 43; movement habits 92; movement patterns 66, 67, 92; movement responses 82; movement style 40; *see also* elements of art

"nature object" 5, 63
nature object 88
Neoclassical 41
Netzel, Sally v, xiii, 59
Non-Realistic 43

Of Time and the River 4
The Oldest Living Graduate 4
One to One: Self Understanding Through Journal Writing 147
O'Neill, Eugene xii, 11
organic knowledge of self 51
originality 58
Othello 3
Our Town 32

Passenger Pigeons 97
"performance acting" 9
"personality actors" 31
personality traits 105
Phenomena Astral Signal 91
physical handicaps 45
physical responses 67, 100
physical spaces 32
Picasso, Pablo 2, 3, 52
playwright's intention 75
plot line 74
"poor theatre" 18
Post-Modern 43
posture and body stance 45
process of self-examination 33
props 75
proxemics 23
psychological attitudes 39
psychological motivations 93

Realistic 43, 75
receptivity 56
Reitz, Dana 40, 41
Respect for Acting 148
Restoration dramas 57
ritual dances 25
rhythm study 63
rhythmic differences 27
rhythmic forces 25, 31
rhythmic patterns 23, 24, 31
rhythmic phrases 69
rhythmic sense 27
Richardson, Don 13, 19
Romeo and Juliet 18
Rouault 2, 3, 52
Royal Hunt of the Sun 35
Ruth Taylor Theatre 2

Satie, Eric 85, 86
Second Harvest 149
self-analysis 22
self-awareness 19, 148
self-discovery 146
"sense memory" 18, 147
Shaffer, Peter 35
Shakespeare, William 3, 27, 67
Shakespearean plays 57
shaman 25
shapes 66
shaping 45
Song of Myself 35
soundtrack of character 65
speech patterns 57
Spoon River Anthology 119, 120, 122, 123, 124, 125, 127, 128, 129, 130, 131
stage decoration 75
stage design 75
stage dressing 75
Stanislavski, Constantin xiii, 4, 10, 20, 32, 50, 51, 52, 147
Stanislavski Method 17, 18, 19, 38
Stanislavski System 17, 18, 20
Stecker, Elizabeth Wear 2
Strasberg, Lee 18

stream of consciousness
writing 65
A Streetcar Named Desire 18, 58
Strindberg, August 76, 97, 98,
99, 106
surrealism 43
symbolism 75

tactile stimulus 47
The Ten Line Exercise ix, 20, 50,
59, 60, 82, 92, 95, 100, 105,
106, 107, 111, 112, 119, 143, 145;
the choice study 51, 59, 67, 68,
97, 100, 117; the movement
study 59, 66, 67, 69, 92, 96, 99,
100, 101, 105, 116, 146; the
sound study 59, 64, 65, 69, 76,
81, 83, 84, 85, 105, 114, 115; the
ten line study 68, 101, 105, 107,
118, 146; the word study 50, 59,
61, 62, 68, 69, 76, 105, 112, 115;
the visual study 55; 65, 66, 69,
87, 90, 115
tension 38
textural composition 65
Theatre of the Absurd 43, 75
The Theatrical Event 37
Time magazine 4
To the Actor 22, 107
traditional theatre 2
Trinity University xiii, 2, 20, 143
Trois Gymnopedies 85, 86

unconscious 21
unconscious visual responses 66

University Interscholastic
League 119
use of color 75

visual image 82, 90
visual information 75
visual memory 38
vocal inflections 105
vocal patterns 93
vocal technique 57
vocal work 57

Whitman, Walt 35
Wilde, Oscar 27
Wilder, Thornton 32
Williams, Tennessee 35, 131, 132,
133, 134
Wilson, Robert 99
Wolfe, Thomas 4
word list 61
work actions 93
work in progress 61
working methods 146, 148
Wright, Frank Lloyd xii, 3 4, 20,
52

Yale University 2
*Your Mythic Journey: Finding
Meaning in Your Life Through
Writing and Storytelling* 148

zero position 95